WHAT WAS THE HIPSTER?

WHAT WAS
THE HIPSTER?
A SOCIOLOGICAL INVESTIGATION

Edited by Mark Greif, Kathleen Ross, and Dayna Tortorici

Transcribed by Avner Davis

n+1 RESEARCH BRANCH SMALL BOOKS SERIES #3

n+1 Foundation
NEW YORK

Published 2010 by n+1 Foundation

68 Jay Street, Ste. 405

Brooklyn, New York

www.nplusonemag.com

Printed by the Sheridan Press

Manufactured in the United States of America

Second Printing.

CONTENTS

PREFACE

ALL DESCRIPTIONS OF hipsters are doomed to disappoint, because they will not be the hipsters you know. Yet someday when hipsters no longer walk the earth, and subcultures have changed, and new aesthetics have evolved, with new terms of disapprobation and praise, the hipster of the period 1999–2010 will remain of historic interest — and investigators at a later date will be at the mercy of whether or not we chose to record our impressions today.

I am reminded of a liberty a friend once took with me. "Have you ever heard of Ali G?" he asked. "No," I answered. "Great, just listen to me do his routines — my impression of him's *perfect*."

Those of you who have encountered hipsters in real life, in other words, may surely complain of the characterizations in this book. But to those of you who are reading this in 2050, I can only say: Everything in this book is true, and its impressions are perfect.

T HE PURPOSE OF *What Was the Hipster?: A Sociological Investigation* is to find out if it is possible to analyze a subcultural formation while it is still happening, from the testimony of people who are close to it. We used the collective knowledge of a very idiosyncratic group of people: readers of and writers for the journal *n+1*, plus interested strangers, at a panel held at the New School; then, after the event, journalists and other critics to whom we gave the early transcripts, so they could challenge our approach and disagree.

Participants were welcome to exploit their own immediate experience and knowledge, their scholarly and analytic inclinations, and whatever bad motives and resentments they no doubt harbored toward ex-neighbors, rivals, or people who dress better or more expensively, to add to a record of a single stereotype and bogeyman — the modern hipster — who has environed us all for more than ten years, at the precise instant that this figure may be changing.

The metamorphosis of the "hipster" — if it is real — involves a word that has been used for insult and abuse gaining a neutral or even positive estimation in the culture. It accompanies the sense that hipster fashion has entered the mainstream as a set of style accessories repackaged for purchase in shopping malls across America, but also that the deeper social impulses that helped create the hipster — as well as the vitally necessary impulses to impugn hipsters — have gone global, mushrooming in Europe and Latin America, too.

It is not possible to say that the hipster is dead — perhaps you know some, perhaps you've seen them eat and sleep — but the fact that one begins to hear visitors to cafes in Williamsburg or on the Lower East Side describe themselves or their friends as "sort of hipsters, you know," suggests it may be time to round up the original target's early history, and the word's original hostile meanings, before it is too late.

"HIPPIE" — A TERM of abuse invented by hipsters or beatniks of the postwar generation for "little hipsters," who just liked to dance and smoke pot but knew nothing about jazz or politics or poetry—became available to mass media in the mid-1960s, thus attracting new, young converts to the lifestyle, until the different sorts of younger people now correctly called "hippies" (who had known themselves as "freaks," or "heads," or possessed no name) accepted it, too, and even found it useful as an identifier ("You dig, it's like a *hippie* shirt.").*

---

* This, anyway, is the story familiarly told. See Charles Perry, *The Haight-Ashbury: A History* (New York: Random House, 1984), 5-6, a pop account

(CONTINUED ON NEXT PAGE)

Could we be at a point with the hipster as significant as that one? Presumably not. Surely a subcultural moniker can't be of immense importance twice. The word hipster comes out of the distant American past, as the name for a previous, truly significant subculture. A main line of our investigation into contemporary hipsters takes up the central concern of that earlier figure, the 1940s and 1950s-era hipster — namely, race, as blackness and whiteness, source of knowledge and ground of resistance, from before the Civil Rights era through our supposedly post-racial era — and asks how the old name came to be taken up again.

Hipsterism as an identifiable phenomenon also very clearly has to do with particular fashions, and fashion micro-trends, which are notoriously hard to explain. The question of which exterior markers are

---

(CONTINUED FROM PREVIOUS PAGE)

based on an impressive wealth of interviews with key protagonists. One additional description from Perry of early, pre-1965 "hippie" derogation and style may be notable because of its surprising echoes with the charges against modern hipsters: "Another grievance was that while Beats were always down and out, the hippies seemed to have money. . . . What was unique to hippies was their attitude — an expansive, theatrical attitude of being cool enough to have fun. They called themselves dudes and ladies rather than cats and chicks. Unlike Beats in their existential black and folkies in their homespun and denim, they wore flashy Mod clothes. . . . Hippies were scattered around in other places in the country, too [besides San Francisco, their birthplace], mostly near college campuses." This certainly sounds a lot like present-day hipsters, and it clearly precedes the later identification of hippiedom with the politics of the anti-war and peace movements.

essential to the hipster, and where they came from and what they mean, clearly drives people most to distraction in these pages. Yet one begins to get hints, thereby, of what is at stake in matters of distinction, and self-love, and superiority around such differences — and, maybe more importantly, how supposedly inexplicable fashion details (like the trucker hat or "ironic" T-shirt), at their origins, actually signified very obvious, precise, and near-articulate things about who one fantasized oneself to be, or apologized for, or envied — especially as these fashions duplicated elements of the past, allowing forms of communication and reinforcement of ideology. Thus fashion details may be more explicable than they seem. One begins to wonder if, more generally, the claim of their arbitrariness is a matter of mystification, and a refusal to trace them to their first wearers or proponents.

We proceeded in our investigations as follows. On a Saturday afternoon in spring 2009, an initial symposium and discussion took place, announced in advance and advertised to the public, at the New School in Manhattan. This book reprints the original papers offered for discussion — though the centerpiece of this book is clearly the lengthy floor debate and discussion that followed. We have resisted the impulse to correct mistakes by the panelists (though a few factual errors are annotated).

Two of the more extensive reportorial accounts of the event follow, in a section called "Dossier," giving a feeling for how the effort was initially received. In the months after the panel, the editors sent transcripts to commentators who we believed might question or dispute the proceedings so far, opening the topic up in new ways. The section with their remarks is titled "Responses." At this point, the organized investigation should spill over into the reader's domain — you, the reader, will have your own sense of where an inquest into the hipster will need to go next, and where you, yourself, disagree. A final section of "Essays," however, offers more considered and detailed articles on particular sub-topics of the field, or expansions into the hipster's contact with the world beyond him — taking up the hipster Other (a.k.a. the "douchebag"), hipster race, hipster gender, hipster aesthetics, and the hipster future.

FOR ONCE, HERE is analysis of a cultural phenomenon not learned from TV, or pre-digested. Thank god for that: when one investigates the record of any subculture, one sees how thoroughly past moments get summed up and misrepresented by intellectual annexations, money-making efforts, second-order media replicas, and latecomers. As if hipsters were Norman Mailer, the hippies were Woodstock, punk were the Sex Pistols, or grunge were Kurt Cobain! Yet each of these manufactured phenomena, because of their superior access to wider publicity strategies and capital (and *film*, crucially, alongside recorded music the most important medium of subcultural transfer), became instrumental in the reproduction of genuine impulses of resistance and hope across generations.

At the same time, neither are the contributors' accounts purely subjective or "on the scene" — far from it, and anyone implicated in the hipster circles spotlighted here will surely detest these contributors as latecomers, spoilsports, and intellectualizers. I believe, having read the texts carefully, that these contributions do converge on a true accounting of the hipster phenomenon, from a certain remove. They try out definitions based on what we've experienced so far, and test historical phases, and mount up possible characteristics — not to mention putting together a king's ransom of rumors and stories and historical facts (or pseudo-facts) that should go into any time capsule of the hipster moment.

I also see that these accounts converge on areas of common blindness. These gaps, as often as not, reflect social conditions of the hipster phenomenon itself — including the persistent inability, despite the centrality of women in every sphere of fashion, art, and endeavor touched by hipsterism, to place the "hipster feminine," or to think about hipster women beyond the filter of male domination of the category.

Though these contributions are meant to be diagnostic, each one must be acknowledged as symptomatic, too, reflecting unconscious attitudes, flaws, vanities, and errors, which can add to the picture of what it once meant to speak of hipsters, in a climate of constant criticism and secret identification. When people sound like asses, we've pretty much allowed them to do so, and you will hear in these pages a certain amount of braying.

The authorities missing in this account, I regret to say, are professional social scientists. The study of the hipster, as opposed to the punk, hippie, raver, goth, cyber-utopian, or b-boy, has not yet drawn its scholars — or else they're in the long and thankless stage of dissertation fieldwork, rather than on faculties where they can be easily located. Naturally, the best thinking that underlies these contributions, though, comes from the written insights of sociologists, anthropologists, urbanists, and geographers, whom literary people must read to understand the world we live in. Thus the slight presumption of the subtitle, *A Sociological Investigation.*

When I describe this project to people who think hipsters are just fashion victims or something fun, I say its purposes are social-scientific. When I talk to people who are more serious, I sometimes describe it as a parody of academic proceedings. It deliberately lacks the "rigor" (as professors say), or formality, of a university undertaking; but it is meant to let people's lives in — to show that the ludicrous can be studied, and, equally, that the serious and academic can be ludic, playful, ordinary.

The anti-intellectualism of American pleasure reading (and the formal requirements of quantification and literature reviews for academia) seem to keep social-scientific books off the hip reading lists of friends. The work of sociology just about everyone discussed in these pages ought to read and experience, as a kind of required generational exercise in self-criticism, is Pierre Bourdieu's *Distinction* (1979). For strategic and professional reasons, Bourdieu targeted that book to high-intellectual cadres in university circles — and the buy-in required for understanding included a quantity of new vocabulary and mental labor usually only encountered in academic philosophy. This little book of ours, on its best reading, will, I hope, send interested parties back to that literature — to Bourdieu, of course, but also to key popular social scientists in our time who have written a crossover literature of wide influence and importance: Barbara Ehrenreich, Thomas Frank, Arlie Russell Hochshild, David Harvey, Juliet Schor, Mike Davis, and others whose names can be found in the bibliography at the back of these pages.

ONE LAST THING. A number of people have sniggered — non-participants and participants both (you'll hear their teasing in the debate transcript) — at the idea of *n+1*, "a journal of literature, intellect, and politics" founded in New York in 2004 (and physically produced in the hipster neighborhoods of the Lower East Side and then Dumbo), initiating a highbrow discussion of hipsters. Partly the challenge is that the topic seems too stupid and demeaning. One of our readers emailed us as soon as the panel was announced, to say: "Is this a joke? If it isn't, that's very, very sad." For others, the trouble was that it was *too much like us* — this challenge is one of what the sociologist would call "inadequate reflexivity." The charge is that *n+1* is *itself* a hipster journal, and molded by the same social forces. I think the former is false, the latter true. The hipster represents, in a deep way, a tendency we founded the magazine to combat; yet he exists on our ground, in our neighborhood and particular world, and is an intimate enemy — also a danger and temptation.

Having read these proceedings, responses, and essays many times now, I think I've learned the following: The hipster represents what can happen to middle class whites, particularly, and to all elites, generally, when they focus on the struggles for their own pleasures and luxuries — seeing these as daring and confrontational — rather than asking what makes their sort of people entitled to them, who else suffers for their pleasures, and where their "rebellion" adjoins social struggles that should obligate anybody who hates authority.

Or, worse: the hipster is the subcultural type generated by neoliberalism, that infamous tendency of our time to privatize public goods and make an upward redistribution of wealth. Hipster values exalt political reaction, masquerading as rebellion, behind the mask of "vice" (a hipster keyword). Hipster art and thought, where they exist, too often champion repetition and childhood, primitivism and plush animal masks. And hipster anti-authoritarianism bespeaks a ruse by which the middle-class young can forgive themselves for abandoning the claims of counterculture — whether punk, anti-capitalist, anarchist, nerdy, or '60s — while retaining the coolness of subculture. It risks turning future avant-gardes into communities of "early adopters."

But I see I'm getting ahead of myself — anyway, it's the universal instinctive hatred of hipsters (even among hipsters!) that makes me believe things will be fine, if we could just see things more clearly — and I may be prejudicing the case.

Enjoy.

– MG

SYMPOSIUM

INTRODUCTION

The following symposium took place on April 11, 2009, at the New School University in New York City, in the Vera List Center, before an audience of 175.

WELCOME, EVERYONE. I want to thank you all for coming out. I hope it'll be a good way to spend a rainy afternoon.

The format today is straightforward. There will be three statements of about ten minutes each. We'll then open the floor to questions, and also arguments. If you have something to say, please say it. At the end of your remark, please say your name, so you can be identified clearly. The discussion should be the heart of the event. We hope to publish it with ideas properly attributed to people. I hope we can build up some kind of historical account so that I, at least, can come out less confused and at the mercy of this topic than when I came in; maybe other people want that too.

In the floor discussion, please do take the opportunity to answer each other. We'll just beg your patience to make sure that it's getting on tape. Okay?

4

POSITIONS

I'M GOING TO SEE IF I can offer possible definitions, based on what I read, and hear, and have seen. Maybe these can form a starting place for discussion. The key thing will be, where these definitions are wrong, to correct them.

Periodization. When we talk about the contemporary hipster, we're talking about a kind of cross-subcultural figure who emerges by 1999 and enjoys a fairly narrow but robust first phase of existence from 1999 to 2003. At which point the category of hipster seemed about to dissipate and return to the primordial subcultural soup, for something else to take over. Instead what we witnessed was an increasing spread and durability of the term, in an ongoing second phase from 2003 to the present.

Genesis. The matrix from which the contemporary hipster emerged included that 1990s culture which the sociologist Richard Lloyd called "neo-bohemia" in his ethnography of Wicker Park in Chicago — that is, a culture of artists who primarily work in bars and coffee shops and rock clubs, while providing an unintentional milieu for "late capitalist" commerce in design, marketing, web development, and the so-called "experience economy" — and also the '90s culture called "indie" or "indie rock."

From about 1980 forward, we possess a strong sense, I think, of how a sequence of new subcultures emerged as alternatives to the successful "subculturation" of consumer capitalism. This sequence began in the diffusion of an ethos associated with punk and DIY. It produced a music of "post-punk," freighted with ideas of the "alternative" and "independent," as separately existing fields of personal and economic activity, culminating in 1991. 1991 is remembered, because of a famous documentary, as "the year punk broke" — which was to say both that it broke into the mainstream, as the most successful post-punk bands moved to corporate labels, and that its spirit was broken on the shoals of mass commercialism. This was encapsulated in the short heyday of "grunge," originally the most local of local scenes, until its overhyped representative figure, Kurt Cobain, finally killed himself from some of these contradictions in 1994.

So the contemporary hipster seems to emerge out of a thwarted tradition of youth subcultures, subcultures which had tried to remain independent of consumer culture, alternative to it, and been integrated, humiliated, and destroyed.

There is also a question of overt politics. Where hipsterdom is taken to be anti-political, it seems that the watershed moments it particularly jeers at, and may have been shaped and periodized by, were two major episodes of ultimately failed political action, which stand out in the political sensibility of this generation: the 1999 protests at the WTO Ministerial conference in Seattle — hence the hipsters' sometime mockery, sometimes embrace, of global labor concern and environmentalism — and the ignored 2003 protests against the promised invasion of Iraq. Barack Obama's election in 2008 then seems to have represented a reunification of the apathetic and the committed around disgust with the previous presidency — *no one* liked George W. Bush.

Localization. It's characteristic of the post-1999 "hipster" moment that it's strongly associated with neighborhoods in cities across the United States that represented either new zones of white recolonization of ethnic neighborhoods or subcolonies of established bohemian neighborhoods. In New York, you only have to say "the Lower East Side" or "Williamsburg" to conjure post-1999 hipsterism, where the residents who were displaced were Hispanic and Jewish. As of 2009, Bushwick seems to be the active locale.

Robert Lanham's 2003 *The Hipster Handbook* describes the North American system in that year: the Plateau in Montreal, College and Clinton in Toronto, Jamaica Plain in Boston, Capitol Hill in Seattle, Whittier in Minneapolis, Echo Park and Silverlake in LA, the Inner Mission in San Francisco, and so forth.

Differentiae. The question becomes: what was it about the turn-of-the-century moment that made this character emerge specifically, and why was it so clear — as I think it *was* clear — that the character had to have *this* name, the hipster, which was so freighted with historical meaning? Subculture has never had a problem with neologism or exploitation of slang: from emo to punk to hippie. But the hipster was someone else already. Specifically, the hipster was a black subcultural figure of the late 1940s, best anatomized in an essay by Anatole Broyard in 1948 (in the period before Broyard began passing for white). This hipster also figures crucially in Ralph Ellison's *Invisible Man.* Then the hipster was a white subcultural figure of the 1950s, explicitly defined by the desire of a white avant-garde to disaffiliate from whiteness, and achieve the "cool" knowledge and exoticized energy, and lust, and violence, of black Americans. The clichéd reference here is to Norman Mailer's essay "The White Negro" of 1957.

The hipster, both in black and white incarnations, in his essence had been about superior knowledge — what Broyard, in his article, called *a priorism*. Broyard insisted that black hipsterism was developed from a sense that black people in America were subject to decisions made about their lives by conspiracies of power which held a monopoly on information and knowledge that they *could never* possibly know. The "hip" reaction was to insist, purely symbolically, on forms of knowledge which you, the black knower, possessed before anyone else, and in fact before the creation of positive knowledge — *a priori*. Broyard focused on the password language of hip slang. So this symbolic knowledge functioned either as self-assertion or as compensation.

Why would "hipster," this archaic term of the '50s, be on everyone's lips at the turn of the 21st century? To answer this, I'd like to introduce my three possible definitions of the contemporary hipster, in his or her emergence and persistence. All three have this quality of *a priorism* built in. (I should preface this with a reminder that when "hipster" is used in a contemporary frame, it is always pejorative. This is not a term people apply to themselves. But neither is it an all-purpose put-down: its contours are very specific.) If subcultures have always known snobs, and collectors, and connoisseurs, the character of the hipster's claim to knowledge may be somehow different.

I think the reason the attribution of hipsterness is always pejorative is that "hipster" is actually identifying today a *subculture* of people who are already *dominant*. The hipster is that person, overlapping with declassing or disaffiliating groupings — the starving artist, the starving graduate student, the neo-bohemian, the vegan or bicyclist or skate punk, the would-be blue-collar or post-racial individual — who in fact aligns himself *both* with rebel subculture *and* with the dominant class, and opens up a poisonous conduit between the two.

DEFINITIONS

Definition 1. This is the originating hipster as "the white hipster." This is by far the most limited definition, and it really applies to what captured me as *different* in the Lower East Side of 1999. Let me enunciate a string of keywords: trucker hats; undershirts called "wifebeaters," worn as outwear; the aesthetic of basement rec-room pornography, flash-lit Polaroids, fake wood paneling; Pabst Blue Ribbon; "porno" or "pedophile" mustaches; aviator glasses; Americana T-shirts for church socials, et cetera; tube socks; the late albums of Johnny Cash, produced by Rick Rubin; and tattoos. *Vice* magazine, which moved to New York from Montreal in 1999; the hipster branding-consultancy-cum-sneaker store called Alife, which started in 1999; American Apparel, the socially conscious, jersey-knit-pajamas-as-clothing, basement-pornographic boutique chain that also started in 1999. These were the most visible emblems of a small and surprising subculture, where the source of *a priori* knowledge seemed to be an only partly nostalgic suburban *whiteness*, the 1970s culture of white flight from the cities to the suburbs, of the so-called "unmeltable ethnics," Irish, Italian, Polish, and so forth, but now with the ethnicities scrubbed off — recolonizing urban neighborhoods with a new aesthetic. As the "White Negro" had once fetishized blackness, the "white hipster" fetishized the violence, instinctiveness, and rebelliousness of lower-middle-class suburban or country whites.

Definition 2. The second possible definition, though, for modern hipsterism: that which belongs to "hipster culture." In the realm of the traditional arts, what would this be? The most commonly offered options seem to be, in literature, the early Dave Eggers, of *A Heartbreaking Work of Staggering Genius* and the early *Believer*. In cinema, the films of Wes Anderson, *Rushmore* and *The Royal Tenenbaums*. I realize these get quite controversial.

"Hipster" culture on *this* definition seems to speak primarily to works of art where the tensions of the work revolve around the very old dyad of knowingness and naïveté, adulthood and a child-centered world — but with a radical or vertiginous alternation between the two. Formally, there is a radicalization and aestheticization of the mode of pastiche, which Frederic Jameson identified in the early '80s as a characteristic mode of postmodern narrative. Here, however, "blank irony" has given way to a reconstruction of past aesthetics and techniques more perfect than the originals, in an irony without sarcasm, without bitterness or critique; reflexivity is used purely to get back to emotion, especially in the drive toward childhood.

In pop music, it gets quite difficult to say whether there is music of any significance made by hipsters, and it's tempting, especially looking from New York, to pick out something like the quickly self-demolishing band the Strokes — who would belong more to hipster definition #1. Dave Eggers briefly tried to ally himself with the Flaming Lips as the right musical companion to *McSweeney's* — hipster definition #2. But if you believe the logic of definition #2, in the perfect pastiche as a mode of recovering the deep feelings of childhood, then the major progenitor band would probably be Belle and Sebastian, even though, Scottish and unconflicted as they are, their origins seem totally outside this system. I'm worried you're going to drop me right there, but, you know, it's a thought.

I should also add that *n+1* has on occasion been called a hipster publication. The reasons remain obscure.

Definition 3, and the one with which I think I might get the most traction. The "hipster" is the name for what we might call the "hip consumer" or what Tom Frank used to call the "rebel consumer." The hipster is by definition the person who does not create real art. If he or she produced real art, he could no longer be a hipster. It has long been noticed that the majority of people who frequent bohemia are what are sometimes called hangers-on or poseurs, art aficionados rather than art producers. The hipster is the cultural figure of the person, very possibly, who now understands consumer purchases within the familiar categories of mass consumption (but still restricted from others) — like the right vintage T-shirt, the right jeans, the right foods for that matter — to be *a form of art*.

What else might mark such a person off from the old and immemorial line of snobs and slummers is the puzzling part. I take it that "hipster" as a name points to the fact that something has become even *more* drastic, or set apart, again, about these people's status as possessors of knowledge; and that, if we believe there is something essential about 1999 that lasts to the present, it is that the acquisition and display of taste before anyone else has also been radicalized, by the new forms of online capitalism; so that it is increasingly hard to possess, for example, popular music that everyone else can't also immediately possess after widespread internet use. The 2009 hipster becomes the name for that person who is a savant at picking up the tiny changes of consumer distinction and who can afford to live in the remaining enclaves where such styles are picked up on the street rather than, or as well as, online.

I suspect those definitions are wrong, but I offer them for what they're worth. I hope they will form a basis for conversation.

I WAS WRONG

After Charles Bernstein

I AM NOT NOW nor have I ever been a hipster. No member of my family, no close friend, no enemy, no rival, no lover, no teacher, no coworker, no classmate, no bandmate, no client, no barkeep, no dance partner, no party guest, no doctor, no lawyer, no broker, no banker, no artist, no singer, no guitar player, no DJ, no model, no photographer, no author, no editor, no pilot, no stewardess, no actor, no actress, no television personality, no robber, no cop, no priest, no deacon, no nun, no hooker, no pimp, no acquaintance known to me has ever been a hipster. Indeed, I have never met a hipster. I deny that there ever existed any such thing. I deny this categorically, and I denounce the very category. I despise it.

So it is that I come before you today to denounce myself, to apologize to the public and to beg your forgiveness. For I have been party to a massive fraud, one that lingers to this very day, though in a diminished and sclerotic form. The fraud held that there were people called hipsters who followed a creed called hipsterism and existed in a realm known as hipsterdom. The truth was that there was no culture worth speaking of, and the people called hipsters just happened to be young and, more often than not, funny-looking.

I entered this fraud voluntarily, at some times delusional, at other times motivated solely by the desire for personal gain, to attract attention to myself, and to alleviate massive credit card debt. For example, on May 11, 2007, I received the following email from an editor at a popular weekly magazine:

Hello Christian,

I'm writing to commission an essay from you for an upcoming cover package devoted to killing off the Hipster, once and for all. We think it'll be an attention-getting issue, and a perfect fit for your sensibility. (I happened to come across an old review of *The Life Aquatic* and thought you'd be perfect.)

In short, our premise is that hipsters—those too-cool kids who snarkily reduce everything to kitsch—have retarded cool. Years ago, they took over Williamsburg, with a legitimately fresh look, but now every 18-to-34-year-old is wearing a faded GI

Joe T-shirt, playing bingo ironically and listening to bands on Matador and Thrill Jockey. What started as an organic, cheeky, post-modern lifestyle is now a carbon copy of a copy — co-opted by Urban Outfitters and sold like fast food.

This was true years ago, but it still hasn't abated. Your essay would wonder, when everything cool in an urban context automatically gets subsumed by now uncool hipsterism, how can anything be cool again? How can cool recover?

We'd need 1,000 words

Deadline: May 18 (or 21, if need be)

Payment: $2,000

Our editor-in-chief would love to talk more with you about the package. Let me know if there's any interest.

Thank you for your consideration.

Sincerely,

[Name withheld]

Such flattery! And such a high word rate! How can cool recover? And how can one go on looking in the mirror every morning after using the word "cool" as a noun? But let's keep our cool.

At their behest, I executed the assignment. It was published, a letter appeared in the next issue saying that the article was useful for picking up dog feces, and a few months later I was paid.

This of course was not the first time I had written lies about hipsters. I had previously published — on the website of the magazine sponsoring this panel — reviews of several movies directed by individuals I erroneously described as hipsters adhering to a hipster aesthetic. I confess to making and now recant in full the following claims:

1. That "the problem with hipsters" is what "happens when a generation refuses to grow up."

This was a misjudgment. Not growing up — that is, the refusal to put away childish things and indeed to maintain and affirm one's inner child, even to the extent that it may blossom into an outer child, though with the wrinkled face of a seeming adult — this is in no sense a problem. Childhood is the only source of authenticity in America. It is America's greatest and most glorious invention — our gift to the world. Permanent childhood is the ultimate form of maturity.

2. That our generation had yet to produce either any lasting artistic achievements or even a decent serial killer on par with Charles Manson.

Here I was wrong on two counts.

Firstly, every single artwork created in the current era is guaranteed by recent technological developments to last forever — to attest permanently to its own artisticness and to inspire infinite artistic regeneration and proliferation. All art is now great art.

Secondly, in evaluating the achievements of murder among those I erroneously identified as hipsters, I neglected to consider two epochal events. As Gus Van Sant's film *Elephant* illustrated, had the perpetrators of the Columbine massacre sublimated their homicidal impulses, their destiny may well have been to move to Williamsburg. And further, to adopt a global view, the perpetrators of the 9/11 attacks fall roughly within the demographic under consideration today. It was often said after the events that the terrorists, by destroying the World Trade Center, had destroyed irony itself. But as the years have passed and the concept of blowback has gained wider recognition, we have come to understand that irony did not die in 9/11. Rather, irony perpetrated 9/11.

3. That hipsters exist in a state of perpetual luxuriant slumming and that rich people and people who grew up poor colluded in a group project of class confusion, conspiring to blur class boundaries temporarily in order to allow themselves to socialize and sleep with each other.

This was a blatant lie. As we all know, there is no such thing as a class structure in America. While there may be mild disparities among us in terms of wealth and status, we the people, as our founding documents mandate, are all created equal, we enjoy equal opportunities, and by the time we reach the age of 25, no matter the circumstances of our birth, we all enjoy the same level of attractiveness to the opposite sex, which, on a scale of one to ten, would be a seven. As Laurie Anderson sings, Let X = X.

4. That hipsters, mostly white (the pastiest of whites), prided themselves on having ethnic friends, that they considered themselves "post-racial," and that when they told racist jokes they were being post-racist.

This was inaccurate. I had neglected to notice that racism in America effectively expired during the 1990s, the decade of Bill Clinton, O. J. Simpson, Rodney King, and Vanilla Ice. Anything that might seem like racism today is merely a sign of nostalgia for our naughty past.

5. That the Age of Twee was finally over.

This was my attempt to bury once and for all Wes Anderson and Belle and Sebastian. To my surprise, both of them returned. Anderson's characters had abandoned the thrift-store dresses and corduroys for designer suits. Belle and Sebastian released new albums with obviously higher production values than their earlier works. Tweeness not only survived and thrived but became highly lucrative. I meanwhile continued to be broke. I haven't bought any new clothes since 2005.

6. That hipsters were disgusted by anything erotic and had little use for the concept of love.

Here I was blind to contemporary realities, for it is obvious to all of us here — and to all of our ex-girlfriends or ex-boyfriends — that the past decade has been the most glorious decade love has ever known. Eros attained powers never imagined by our greatest romantic poets. Lovers burst through shrouds of anonymity into instantaneous fits of impassioned eloquence. Arousal infested our apartments like mice. Telephone poles never seemed so tumescent. There were so many people to meet, and eventually so many people to break up with. Luckily you could just text them, and if you felt bad about it, text them again later to meet up. Love was like a lottery that everybody won. It was so beautiful that sometimes you even missed being lonesome.

7. That hipsterism was simply the aftermath of suburban childhood and that its expiration in one's mid-thirties presented the hipster with two horrifying options: marriage, procreation, and a bloated return to suburbia; or life in the city as an aging hipster.

This was a falsehood. As my hero, the critic Lee Siegel, recently argued in the *Wall Street Journal*, the life of a nuclear family in an American suburb is an unalloyed ecstasy. I remember my own suburban childhood. I spent many hours every summer day throwing a tennis ball against the door of my barn in a vain attempt to train myself to be an infielder. By the time I was 13, I had learned to ride a bike — I'm a slow learner. I was gently mocked by my youth basketball teammates for wearing Brooks brand basketball sneakers, rather than Reeboks or Nike Airs. "Did you get those shoes at the pharmacy?" they asked. "No, my mom got them," I said. I joined the Cub Scouts but dropped out after the den mother's son pushed me to the ground and administered several running jumping knee slams to my stomach, causing me to cry. These experiences build character, and without them I would not be in front of you today. Oh, what a paradise it was.

8. That there might emerge a hipster pro-life movement.

I did not actually mean this when I said it, but I realized I should never have even uttered the notion when I saw the movie *Juno*. I am now of the opinion that procreation should be prohibited before the age of 30, except among the rich and in Alaska.

9. That the hipster had transformed into the Indie Yuppie, which we might imagine as the fusion of Kurt Cobain and Adam Gopnik.

Here I experienced a failure of imagination. What would have happened to Kurt Cobain if he had pulled through his depression and come out the other end to experience the joys of fatherhood? He may well have stopped touring, moved his family to a co-op on the Upper West Side, had a few more kids, applied his considerable literary talents to writing prose, mellowed into the drollery of prosperous middle age, developed a taste for smoked mozzarella, and become a *New Yorker* staff writer. In the final analysis, Kurt Cobain and Adam Gopnik are the same person, and all of us are that person, too. Me and you and everyone we know.

10. That hipsterdom would soon be the field of a civil war between the mean hipsters and the nice hipsters.

It is never wise to predict the future, and what has since come to pass is the opposite of what I two years ago predicted. Among the young, the nice people and the mean people joined forces, surrendered all claims to irony and stood as one in support of the man whom they elected our president. I was too busy to register or to vote, but I agreed with them. And soon I came to see that whereas the era I had just lived through, which some call the Aughts and others the Naughts, had elicited only one appropriate response — nihilism — the new era of change we can believe in demands earnestness. And in this new era I am but a pathetic relic. What they used to call a second-rate hipster.

So now I offer you my apology, and I offer it specifically to the young, to those whose twenties are now transpiring. I have heard about you. I have heard that you love the internet and think the future will be just great. I have heard that you are never bored. I have heard that you said one of the best things about cocaine is that if you snort it at a dinner party the mess gets cleaned up really fast. One of you wrote to me yesterday and said this:

> Hipster is a derogatory term for someone who is interested in culture. The term would not exist were the phenomenon [of interest in culture] any more than a scum atop the vast shallow pond of American society. It assumes self-consciousness, deceit, and affectation, because everyone here is so fucking unbelieving that anyone could take unmediated pleasure in art.

> Arf. New York is toxic.

I was that poison. I was the toxic bachelor. Now I will get out of the way, and you can go forth and believe and take your unmediated pleasure. My advice is to stay out of debt.

VAMPIRES OF LIMA

I JUST GOT BACK from a month of touring, a week of which I spent in Mexico City working on a live soundtrack to a new film by Jem Cohen. They were having a retrospective of his work, and he invited Guy Piccioto from Fugazi, T. Griffin, Andy Moor from The Ex, and me to create a live audio counterpart for the film. So basically Jem invited me, but it was the hipsters who invited Jem.

The main guy was quite sweet and efficient, he liked slim-fitting jeans and flannel shirts, knew all the good food spots and had a sense of humor that moved between dry and arid. But after meeting him the thing that lingered in everyone's mind was his mustache. A fantastic thick Mexican mustache which he wore like a tie, facial hair to make Burt Reynolds envious. After a few days there I realized that a handful of the

Mexican hipsters were wearing similarly impressive anachronistic mustaches — these batches of hair that seemed straight out of the 1970s, retro-cool. In America, a lot of these guys would read as gay. But in DF, they were modulating the hipster-historical-irony thing with some of the same markers and some radically different ones. Anyhow, I was talking to him about the city where he lived. And he told me, "My neighborhood is too . . . hipstery. So I'm moving to La Roma." Hipsterism — and its immediate byproduct, hipster antipathy — is now a global phenomenon.

The most adamantly anti-hipster person I ever met was from Lima, Peru. Let's call him "Carlos." I was in Lima last December doing a few gigs, and he was telling me about the hipsters there. Peruvian hipsters are a new phenomenon, less than two years old. Carlos credited the music website Pitchfork as contributing in large part to the birth of the Limeño hipster.

Peruvian hipsterism meant that the middle-class kids who looked down on cumbia music all their lives were suddenly throwing parties and dancing to it — all because of a compilation called "Roots of Chicha: Psychedelic Cumbias from Peru." "Roots of Chicha" was released on a French-run Brooklyn label called Barbès. The cool New York label allowed these kids to see this old music in a new light; it wasn't simple recontexualization, it was an awareness that this poorly dressed and deeply unhip aspect of their Peruvian-ness had

entered into a global conversation — involving guitars, drugs, wacky '70s fashions, tragic plane wrecks,
retro chic. Nowadays the marketing term invented by
Barbès — "cumbias psicodélicas" has entered into the
Limeño hipster lexicon. I was asked to bring a stack
of the "Roots of Chicha" CDs to Lima with me, since
import prices are so expensive there. Thing is, you
can still get a lot of the original cumbias on the Barbès
compilation — and tons more like them — in secondhand
shops around the city. Prices have risen, but it's still
far more affordable than the compilation.

The ungenerous reading is that Peru's hipsters
have too much money and neocolonized brains. These
poor rich kids only value local culture when repackaged by other, cooler countries. Carlos subscribed to
this, and took it a step further by being obsessed with
the teenage daughter of a drug lord in the jungle city
of Iquitos — for him, it didn't get any realer than her.
This girl he'd met in the summer was authenticity
and experience embodied — although he kept falling
asleep as he waited for her to appear online so they
could chat via AIM. Even dangerous sexy jungle realness
requires some intense mediation. Point is, one person's
projection of the hipster births another's phantom of
its opposite. Things can get surreal very quickly, making one long for the good old ironic hipster stance.

Anyhow, I see the Limeño hipsters differently — once they hear that a slice of Peruvian music

has entered into a global stage, it transforms from being a lower-class, uncool, overly localized thing into something open, current, cosmopolitan. Even if you subscribe to the ungenerous reading, the fact is, chicha cumbia bands now have a slightly wider audience. The door is cracked open. One can try to keep pushing and open it up even wider. Because of a cool Brooklyn compilation, a discursive space of sonic if not social possibility has opened up in Lima's richer neighborhoods. You can't hate on that.

Another thing I see illustrated in the anti-hipster worldview is that the rise of the hipster is intrinsically linked to widespread internet use, and the dwindling time in which a fashion moves from an expression of individual style to something photographed, blogged, reported on, turned into a trend, marketed, and sold. The emergence of each global city's hipster can probably be correlated to internet penetration there — the Limeño hipster is new, because internet remains slow and expensive there.

The figure of the hipster is a by-product of increasing digitally mediated self-awareness — the hipster's birth simply registers that we've all gotten a little panoptic. You see it in full effect at social networking sites like Facebook and places like LastNightsParty.com, and you see it at the top-down corporate level — although there isn't much distinction between the two, and that's partly why the hipster exists.

A Chilean friend runs a popular website which features daily street fashion photographs. She's sponsored by a global sneaker brand. This is normal. Other brands probably pay her extra to plant "street" photos modeling their latest gear. Most hipster discussion seems to express nostalgia for a time when there was a substantive difference between underground culture and mainstream culture.

Anyhow, hipsters do look different depending where you are. I have to admit, it was a little bit hard to spot the vampiric Limeño hipsters. They weren't as cool as you kids are, and they don't have a fraction of your purchasing power. In places like North Europe or Dubai the image of the hipster is much closer to something New Yorkers would recognize. Dubai kids are always in London or LA or New York or Tokyo, and the Scandinavians are genetically predisposed for great design sensibility.

I had a strange moment DJing in Graz, Austria a few months ago. The backstage area felt like Bedford Ave — nearly everyone was wearing tight pants, fancy sneakers, colorful T-shirts and hoodies, trucker caps, everything.

And it wasn't just Austrian kids either; there were some friends from Croatia and Slovakia as well. But nothing ever truly flattens — among the non-hipsters in Graz, there were a dozen or so dreadlocked white dudes (without Rastafarian signifiers), and other tragically unhip European subculture types. If you've visited Spain in the past decade, particularly Barcelona, you probably scored a false-positive hipster ID when you saw kids rocking mullets. The Spanish mullets are non-ironic; people have been wearing them, unfashionably, for decades now, well before *Vice España* started up a year ago.

One of the things I wonder most about the figure of the hipster is this: What are we not talking about when we're talking about the hipster? For example, criticizing the hipster is often a way of discussing gentrification and neighborhood change — while exempting oneself from the process. Figured as scapegoats, hipsters ruin neighborhoods by driving up rents with their parental subsidies, while the non-hipsters just . . . live there. Neutral and pleasant. Which is a totally ridiculous conceit.

Of course, a strong anti-hipster stance is an uncool approach, so, as Christian just demonstrated, the question of the hipster is more frequently answered with tongue-in-cheek jokes or irony — which also prevent a useful conversation from emerging. Especially in the gentrification debate. Artists, not hipsters are gentrification's shock troops. And in many cases, before the artists think to move in, the children of a neighborhood's original residents are the ones who first start tinkering with buying houses there and opening up things to a new market, a new income bracket, a new set of amenities. By the time the hipster appears in a neighborhood, the gentrification process is well underway. If anything, the presence of cool independent coffee shops staffed by white waiters with tattoos they can easily cover for a job interview signifies that a neighborhood will soon reach its coolness peak.

I imagine that folks moving to Bushwick open their closets and think "I'm not a hipster, my parents don't pay my rent, I listen to classic country music without a trace of irony," and go on being the same arrogant overprivileged people they were, with a smug satisfaction that it's only hipsters who destroy neighborhoods, not them or their friends. I'm saying talking about hipsters in terms of class isn't enough — the larger, more important narrative is class mobility, or lack of it. Just because you're interning at some magazine for peanuts and trying to live cheaply doesn't make you working class. But the figure of the hipster seems to confuse the realization that we're all complicit in making or ruining civic spaces, by pinning the blame on a straw man in skinny jeans.

DISCUSSION

MARK GREIF: We now move on to the discussion portion of the program. Editor-at-large Allison Lorentzen of *n+1* is going to ask people to speak, and cut them off if they act crazy.

LEAH MELTZER: Mark, you kind of talked earlier about class mobility, and I think you said "a romanticization of the lower-middle class." I was wondering if you could talk more about what that's about.

GREIF: What I had in mind — I was thinking about the oddity of the Norman Mailer moment, when Mailer hates mainstream society, he hates square society, but also he wants a kind of personal energy. In fact, it turns out, he explains, he wants the energy of the orgasm. But once Reichian therapy was out, as an option, it seemed he could only re-acquire the energy of the orgasm by seizing on *black* culture.

What I found interesting in thinking about the white hipster as a figure — when I began asking about these trucker caps and so forth — is that it seemed clear that the people who were part of this first hipster subculture in fact belonged to, I think, originally quite different class positions. People who write about bohemia and about subcultures — such as Robert Lanham, in what I think, even though it's a comedy book, is the best book we have about hipsters, *The Hipster Handbook*, and Robert Lanham is one of our special guests this afternoon [*Lanham stands up in audience*], who will answer your questions, I hope — in his book there's a case made for the existence of, I think they're called "WASHes," I can't remember, but a category of hipsters, people who —

ROBERT LANHAM: The "Waitstaff And Service Hipster."

GREIF: —the waitress and service hipster, there's a case made for them as a standard part of the community: people who are upwardly mobile from the lower-middle class, to an artistic bohemian class, but wind up essentially serving coffee and beers for the people who believe themselves to be downwardly mobile, from the upper middle class. It seems in accounts of bohemia you get these juxtapositions again and again.

Well, what's striking is that *both* class groups in the white hipster moment seem to have that Norman Mailer desire, too: How can you get the *energy* to consume red meat even though you know it's bad for the environment? How do you get the energy to be tough? And it turns out you do it, perhaps, by going back to the imagination of the trailer park, and of Merle Haggard, as somehow embodying the kind of ritual power which you too can have access to — of a lower-class, a white "outlaw" Other.

But the real class mobility question is, ultimately, Jace's question about those who are fixed and can't move anywhere, right?

NICK DELANEY: I hope I can keep the ball rolling by mentioning something that occurred to me which has to do with the economic basis for this stuff. I think when we first think about hipsters in the 1960s or 1950s, when the term originated, and then continuing through the '70s and '80s, it was quite possible to drop out of bourgeois society and get a job at the post office or something like that, and then live a bohemian existence, even in New York City. Now, of course, that's not possible. So I wonder if some of the romanticization of the redneck and all that stuff is a nostalgia for a time when you could drop out of college and say, "Screw that rat race, I'm gonna go be a mail carrier," but being a mail carrier was a job that was easy to get and actually paid pretty well in terms of the purchasing power of those dollars. Whereas I guess I'm making a point that nowadays, if you drop out of bourgeois society, your purchasing power is going to be like one fifth of a yuppie's with elite university credentials. Whereas back then you could drop out and have like two-thirds of the standard of living of a sort of organization man. I wanted to raise those issues.

GREIF: Seems right. This could be a counter-account of white hipster nostalgia: as you said, as a nostalgia for a time when in fact the income distribution was flatter, and the people with whom you were living were of the same social class as you.

ANDREW LEVINE: My question is a response to the earlier part of Jace's discourse, when he gave an account of some of his travels in Latin America. I suppose I should get to the question, first, and then an explanation of what brought it to my mind. The question is: To what extent do you think hipsterism, in both postcolonial powers and former colonized nations, is a way for young people to grapple with the questions raised by postcolonialism?

What brought this up for me was that in my own experiences, folks in countries like France and also former French colonies, in West Africa chiefly, also the Caribbean, "hipsters" — or as they call themselves in French, *branchés* — tend to use artifacts of the colonial era, such as old advertisements from the 1950s made by French companies for broadcast, or for printing in colonial nations, in the same way that American hipsters may focus on things like country music and certain artifacts of suburban living. Or they like going to restaurants which have colonial themes. I'm not sure if anyone has seen this in their own experiences and travels. But: To what extent do you think hipsterism in certain countries is a way for people — young people — to deal with postcolonial issues?

JACE CLAYTON: From my experiences in Latin America, which have been fairly extensive over the past year or fifteen months: not at all, actually. And I think the criticism of hipsters there is that they are American-centric, or very Europhilic. The classic claim about Buenos Aires is that the city has always been the hipster city of Latin America, which is looking to Paris for ideas, to London for ideas. For the folks I was talking with, specifically in Lima, there was all this amazing music — you know, you hear it passing on the micro-buses, you hear it on every street — that was cumbia, but the only moment at which it was actually brought to their attention and sort of entered into their cultural radar was when it was imported, repackaged with a nice booklet written in English, with very colorful photos of people who were national figures thirty years earlier in Peru. So a lot of people see Latin American hipsterism as actually a failure to engage with postcoloniality, and what its possibilities are.

GREIF: What about when you're in France?

CLAYTON: Oh, in France?

GREIF: Yeah, France is weird, right? I remember being in Paris in 1999 and someone . . . what is the French word again for hipster?

LEVINE: They call themselves *branchés.** Some of them just use the English word and say *'eepstair*. They copy a lot of English and American slang words, but the native word they use the most is *branché*, for hipster.

---

* Editor's Note: Subsequent research indicates that the French only seem to say *hipster*, drawing the word directly from American English, and still suggesting an imported phenomenon. *Branché* is an older and more general term, closer to our words "trendy," connected, in the know, etc. A hipper term for *branché* seems to be *branchouille*, representing a recent mutation of pronunciation. The more strictly derogatory French term, approximating our "hipster," is *bobo*: a bobo acts cool but has money, pretends to make art but buys shoes, pretends to be radical but hangs on to privilege. This is drawn from an American coinage by the sinister David Brooks, who supports this hollowing-out of radicalism, contracting the words "bourgeois bohemians" — both, of course, French terms imported in the 19th century into English. Thanks to readers Elizabeth Stark and Cédric Duroux for help with this correction.

GREIF: I remember someone said to me, "Oh we'll take you to the cool bar," and the cool bar's motif, essentially, seemed to be "colonialism in French Indochina," so we would sit in a rickshaw and be served drinks by costumed "Oriental" waiters.

CLAYTON: I don't go to those places. It's true there is a sort of a postcolonial chic — a nostalgia for the days when we were less enlightened.

LEVINE: I think I've actually gone to that bar that Mark is talking about! I was taken to it —

GREIF: Great, there's only one bar like that in all of Europe . . .

LEVINE: That's exactly the sort of thing I was talking about. And they played songs from the 1950s, bad French pop songs romanticizing life in Vietnam or in West Africa or something like that. That's the sort of thing they tack onto there. And I didn't know if it was specific to France, or if it was also specific to Spain or former colonies of Spain or Portugal and such.

CHRISTIAN LORENTZEN: Mark, this reminds me of something from the Norman Mailer "White Negro" essay that you didn't mention, this part of it at the end, as I recall, when he drives toward the concept of miscegenation, while Jim Crow is still in effect, and calls that the great white fear of the time. Do you think that that hope for miscegenation bears any similarity to this idea of postcolonialism?

GREIF: Well . . . Mailer and others, the fancy-pants intellectuals, not that I want to make fun of fancy-pants intellectuals, often have this idea that miscegenation is the one thing that "the evil white people" — as opposed to "me" — are afraid of. Yet from the 1840s on, there's been a very lively fantasy that miscegenation is the only solution to America's racial problem, in part out of a kind of nobility, but often out of, perhaps, the fact that the alternative would be some kind of justice or reparation. Now, the hipsters. Do we believe that, for example, the white hipster — in taking up the trucker cap, belt buckle, and mustache — is steering back toward a culture which would be, in fact, not as class-bound as the increasingly stratified culture, post '70s and '80s? Which would be, as it were, class-miscegenated? This would go very much more toward the earlier conclusion. I don't know. It would be a much more optimistic reading . . .

ALLISON LORENTZEN: Before you guys ask each other any more questions I think we should go back to the gentleman standing by the microphone.

ANDREW PINA: Recently I read a kind of funny *Onion* article with a headline that said something like, "Group of Hipsters Realize Longtime Friend Is Actually Homeless Person," and it went on to say they shopped at the same thrift stores and drank the same beers. . . . It was pretty good. I was wondering what you see as hipsters' or so-called hipsters' relation to actual poor and lower-class people, and how hipsters or anybody are trying to mobilize and help that class of people.

GREIF: [*To audience*] Does anyone have a feeling about this?

DAVE CLOONEY: It seems that both hipster movements (the 1950s and the 1990s) come expressly at a time of, maybe not equally distributed wealth, but of advancing wealth. In the '50s and the early '60s you have the post-war era. Our industrial competitors were destroyed, and that was the first big push of international oil. Tom Wolfe wrote a book called *The Pump House Gang*, where he did a series of essays on a number of different young people, disaffected youth in their twenties, who had more money and less artificial constraints on what they needed to do, and so they were able to do different things like go surfing, go to the Noonday Underground, join the Mod movement in London.

Then once again you have this economic boom, and again it wasn't necessarily evenly distributed, but you have massive amounts of consumer credit that are made available to disaffected twentysomethings, who once again don't have a lot of external constraints — they don't necessarily need to go to a farm, or go to factory work — so it's a consumer movement. There's money to be spent and nothing else really that's being demanded of the mass of youth, for them to do something specific, so they cannibalize older authentic culture to fuel consumerism. It just seems like a natural path at certain points in capitalism. And so the idea that hipsters have anything specific to do with homelessness, or actual social problems, or an actual critique of class issues — it's actually the alternative: to engage in an argument, an endless argument about aesthetics and taste, as opposed to an actual argument about politics and classism.

SAMUEL DWYER: The question I have is, I think that at the core of hipsterism is a certain intellectualism, and if that's true and if *n+1* is a hipster publication, isn't hipsterism, like, the best thing that's happened at the end of the Bush years?

C. LORENTZEN: I would dispute that at the core of hipsterism there is intellectualism. I say this from my living in Williamsburg for two years.

I have found that, whereas often when I lived in other places and I saw someone who seemed like a hipster, they tended to be well read, when I was in Williamsburg, where everyone looked like that, most people didn't, or a lot of people didn't, know a damn thing.

A. LORENTZEN: Can you name the other places where you lived where people were well read?

C. LORENTZEN: Park Slope, Windsor Terrace, Fort Greene, Clinton Hill, Cambridge, Somerville, not necessarily Hopkinton, Massachusetts.

DWYER: But aren't they chasing the same thing?

C. LORENTZEN: No, they were chasing . . . These often were people who worked in the fashion industry.

A. LORENTZEN: When did you live in Williamsburg?

C. LORENTZEN: I moved in in 2005 and left in 2007. There was this incident where I got home around dawn and I tried to open my door but the door handle fell off, then I tried to climb up into my bathroom window, which I had done before by piling up trash cans, and I was somewhat inebriated, so it didn't work very well, and then some of the residents — I lived in this house behind this other house — some of the residents in front, who I either woke up or they were already awake, called the landlord, and he let me in, but after that I was embarrassed, so I figured it would be a good idea to move.

MAUREEN "MOE" TKACIK: I was going to just attempt to draw a greater link between the economic realities of the age and what hipsterism really means. My thinking is that hipsterism — the growth of it, and then the growth of the hipster antipathy movement — essentially, on some level, happened in order to convey to our generation the fallacy or the flaws in deregulation. It was the deregulation of culture.

I think that everyone here, most people in my generation, grew up when our great need, our shortage, the vital commodity that we were missing out on, was not food or, like, energy or minerals, we had all those things, but we really, a lot of us — this is the suburban thing — were missing out on culture.

At that point, and I'm talking about the '90s, there were a lot of barriers to entry, there was a lot of red tape involved, in entering a subculture. It was a slow process. It was bureaucracy-ridden. You had to figure out what zines were, and then find *The Face* magazine — that was a really big step — but if you didn't have that going for you, it was kind of a mystery, and there were all sorts of things you had to figure out.

Then 1999 came along, and subculture was deregulated by the internet, and at first that seemed so awesome, right? Before, if you would enter some sort of subculture, say punk or rockabilly or twee or something like that, there were all sorts of controls on whether or not you could get out of it, there were just limitations, and then suddenly we had this huge throbbing thing that was a little bit nebulous and you didn't really know how to identify anyone except for whether they were wearing American Apparel — and that's sort of another deregulation, because the easy access to credit allowed American Apparel to open like 200 stores in two years, which was really unprecedented in retail.

So my sense is that this was our generation before we actually grew up and a lot of us witnessed the massive intragenerational income gap that occurred because we were like, "Who the fuck needs a three-million-dollar bonus? That's just gratuitous."

And so while it was always a struggle to survive, during 2001 to 2007 or 2008, in New York or Philadelphia or Chicago or wherever, it was definitely feasible. I mean in Philadelphia, everyone started buying houses, and then they could use them as ATMs, as you used to be able to do, I guess. Here, there was always some sort of cool-hunter job that would hire you to do some copywriting that was completely banal. And none of it seemed like any sort of malevolent force. But then, as we found out, allowing that intragenerational income gap to widen all those years, funded by the Chinese — that wasn't a good idea.

And now we know, kind of on a visceral level, what we wouldn't have before — if we hadn't seen hipsters go from people who maybe intimidated us a little bit, maybe because they were cooler, to people who were just completely retarded and too young.

AUDIENCE MEMBER: What was funded by the Chinese, just for clarification?

GREIF: Our debt.

TKACIK: The kind of continued growth of the American economy and accompanying inequality. The dramatic expansion of our financial services sector, to the detriment of every other industry except maybe healthcare.

GREIF: So —

TKACIK: So my question is, would you agree with that?

[*Audience laughter*]

ROB OAKLEY: I have a question about the future of whatever hipsterism was, or hipsterism is now, in relation to America, specifically because I've read Richard Florida's book and everything else about the rise and the flood of the creative class. And kind of like what Jace Clayton said about — I really liked this, what was it? — "Artists are shock troops for gentrification" — so now, after this whole mortgage crisis, are hipsters going to stop being an urban phenomenon and be like squatting in suburbs?

Is it going to be like Omaha and Austin, because everyone has broadband now? Because it's also an issue of access to information, so if the Obama administration is saying we're going to be putting up the new version of the Great Depression grid — everyone's going to have broadband in America — is the future hipster going to be urban, or does that even matter anymore?

CLAYTON: It's a provocative question. I actually like this idea of hipster flight from the city, so suddenly *everyone's* going to be drinking Pabst Blue Ribbon and wearing detachable belt buckles.

OAKLEY: Everyone will just go back to Milwaukee or wherever they're from.

GREIF: Jace, in his piece in *n+1* Number 7, talks a good bit — partly through music but also through culture and economics — about squats across Europe. It's something that I think many of us have wondered about: are artists' squats or squatted communities emerging in the United States, in, for example, Stockton, California, where it seems as if, if you were just a little bit motivated, you could go and set up shop at a newly built house and —

A. LORENTZEN: Stockton, California is the home of Pavement, right?

GREIF: The home of Pavement originally, thus making it all the more appropriate, and also the foreclosure capital of the country, I think, or certainly of California. Are there artists who are setting up entire housing developments as squats? Does anybody know? Are foreclosed houses being squatted by broadband-accessible hipsters? Or artists, I should say?

CLAYTON: It's funny . . . We're talking about artists and doers as the vanguard that hipsters will follow. It's really interesting that one of America's most successful anarchist publishing brands, Crimethinc — you can get their books at the Bowery Poetry Club, their books are franchised at certain coffee shops around the country — they work and live out of a house, sort of a McMansion, somewhere between Oregon and

California. They've been there for a couple years, so if they're leaving, presumably soon, if not already, hipsters will follow.

JOSH STANLEY: My question's going to be kind of speculative. Being a hipster is being treated in the questions and responses as a specific phenomenon, even a specific response to capitalism, or to the particular era we're living in, and interesting because particular. What I wanted to ask is whether there's *nothing* interesting about it, whether it is only one of the necessities of capitalism, as a homogenizing impulse as capitalism expands. I don't think that capitalism past is just one of the ways capitalism can go, I think that this is what capitalism demands, and that the sort of denial of class differences and the denial of registering of particular national or class consciousnesses — which are different — is the evil of capitalism as is. I think I've raised a question, so . . .

GREIF: There are at least two relevant accounts running in these questions and from the presentations. One: hipsterism as the mechanism of the assertion of distinction. Where everyone is trying to distinguish themselves from other people in increasingly trivial ways, thus taking their eye off of essential matters. Two: hipsterdom as homogenizing force, creating a kind of overall "rebel" consumer culture, to which one can belong by saying "I'm opting out," when in fact you're opting in.

STANLEY: The way of perhaps bringing those two together is to say that capitalism converts what are otherwise recognized as qualitative distinctions into quantitative distinctions.

PADDY JOHNSON: The question I had has to do with the use of the term "nostalgia," which has been thrown around a lot today with regard — specifically with regard to cultural consumption. And I'm just wondering, do you guys think nostalgia is the right term for that? Because to me it implies that we would have stopped talking about *Charles in Charge*, but I'm not sure that that conversation ever stopped.

GREIF: Why would nostalgia make you stop talking about *Charles in Charge*?

JOHNSON: I mean isn't there an implication there that you're sort of wishing — there's something in the past that you liked that is no more?

GREIF: Wouldn't that be *Charles in Charge*?

JOHNSON: But it's still around, right? We're still having these conversations. We never really stopped.

C. LORENTZEN: I used to hang out with a guy who would always bring up the sitcom *Gimme a Break!* Eventually I started to avoid him.

GREIF: I don't think that answered the question. I can feel there's like an invisible barrier between us and the questioner — we're totally missing the force of your question. Can someone else answer? Because I feel we're being obtuse.

AUDIENCE MEMBER: Well, is this like the difference between bohemia and neo-bohemia? Everyone keeps saying 1999, and I don't remember what happened then except I graduated high school, but —

GREIF: That's what happened, you graduated from high school.

A. LORENTZEN: That's when I graduated from high school.

AUDIENCE MEMBER: — is that your question [*to Johnson*], where does something stop being irony and become nostalgia?

GREIF: Is that your question? That nostalgia is in fact this long-term, permanent condition . . .

JOHNSON: Yeah, I think that was closer to what I was getting at.

GREIF: I don't know if this will go toward an answer, but a lot of people have noticed the fact that early-phase hipsterism, if we believe there's an early phase, seemed to center on a recollection of the 1970s, and potentially on the styles and dress of Mommy and Daddy when you were born, so that if you say that this thing centered on 1999 and you subtract twenty-five years, then somehow the imagination of 1974, when we came into the world and saw admirable figures who were wearing leisure suits or whatever . . . that moment seems to have provided the style and consciousness of early-phase hipsterism.

Present-day hipsterism, at least as I observe it, seems to be just a recollection of the 1980s, that is, the moment when you were — you're now 25 so Mommy and Daddy were wearing leggings, or leg warmers I guess they're called, and oversized T-shirts and all this kind of stuff.

The worry in that is that when we talk about hipsterism as if it were a quite sophisticated phenomenon, or indeed about "nostalgia," as about things you remember in some quite substantive way — so you remember *Charles in Charge* and . . . was the star of *Charles in Charge* Scott Baio?

WHOLE AUDIENCE: YES!!

GREIF: — You remember Scott Baio and your longing for Scott Baio and your *Tiger Beat* posters on the wall — this all seems like a quite substantive nostalgia, whereas the worry in this movement of hipsterdom, if it should survive, is that in fact it represents a style culture which will only be a longing — decade or half-decade by decade or half-decade, therefore micro-generation by micro-generation, because this seems to be the style that time is measured in now — the longing will just be for whatever the moment of your origination was. Whatever Mommy and Daddy wore because they were real adults when you were tiny.

You find that threatening, right? That's troubling. It's very worrisome to me. This would point toward what we are imagining as "hipsterdom" — as something having substantive commitments to the past — as really just being a kind of infantile desire for the recovery of the identity of former people who were recognizable as strong adults. While we are still weak children. Did that have anything to do with your question?

JOHNSON: I think that answered it.

MANOAH FINSTON: I totally agree with what you just said, and I think that there's a relationship, a curious one, between authenticity and hipsterdom. I think that, for me, there's a certain ambivalence about memory. Every generation, our attention span gets shorter, our memories are shorter in view, and so when you talk about the moment of origination, that people in their twenties are nostalgic for the '80s, sure, because that's what people remember.

But in a way, you could argue then that hipster culture is doing a great service to world culture at large, because people are safeguarding the authenticity of the generation before their own, or the moment before their own.

There's a sense that to be a hipster is to be permanently and obsessively committed to being "for real" — that hipsters are the "real" people and their lives are authentic and that the experiences they're having are meaningful, so if you live in Bushwick in the McKibbin lofts you're "for real" because you have bedbugs and it sucks.

And I'm wondering if this commitment to protecting the authenticity of experiences from a generation before — like the *Tiger Beat* posters and Scott Baio and all this stuff — isn't useful and productive. And I want to argue that it goes against what I think is the usual stigma of hipster culture, which is that it's completely nihilistic — that there's no value except pleasure, that there's no use, that hipsters don't believe in anything, they don't do anything.

So maybe if you look at hipster culture as this positive protective force of our cultural moment, then maybe that is the ultimate merit of hipster culture. So I ask you and anyone else in the room, do you think that therein lies the sort of positive structure and dynamic of hipster culture?

[*Silence from the panel*]

A. LORENTZEN: Do you guys want to respond to the question?

GREIF: I would put that to the audience. Surely there's a positive account. . . . I mean that's a very compelling positive account for the virtue of hipsterism.

BRIAN GALLAGHER: Yeah, but why? It's *crap* that's being remembered. Does it matter if the memory of *Charles in Charge* is protected? And if you try to protect things that are actually worthwhile — like it would be much more square to insist on how great Nirvana was, because they're actually a good band, than it would to insist on how great Debbie Gibson was. That would be more of a hipster thing. So you're necessarily protecting things that are worthless.

C. LORENTZEN: It reminds me of the time I was invited to go see Air Supply at a concert in upstate New York.

I think that a lot of what's done in the preservation of culture, as we see it among the hipsters, of things like *Charles in Charge*, is a stripping of their context, a sort of momentary leering that we do, and then we throw away *Charles in Charge* and move on to Air Supply. And I don't think that it serves a higher purpose.

GREIF: One thing we haven't spoken about is that for people who were politically hopeful at the end of the 1990s, the movement in youth subculture which was occurring simultaneously with this hipster emergence, if you believe me, was the anti-capitalist, anti-globalization movement which everyone remembers. What year is the WTO Ministerial Conference . . . the Battle in Seattle? [*Forgetting own presentation*]

SEVERAL PEOPLE: 1999.

GREIF: 1999! See? Everything happened in 1999! One question which I find very hard to face down, especially when people talk about hipster vegetarians, hipster vegans, is whether there remains a connection between hipsterdom and the long hope for . . . environmentalism as youth subculture, anti-capitalism as youth subculture. Certainly these things have always been woven into the popular music subcultures we think of, with riot grrrl, and what I'm now told are called "crust punks." That's what the young tell me. Jace was actually explaining to me the other day about crust's relation to European teknivals. Do you have a sense of this? Do we believe an attachment remains — a genuine attachment — between hipster culture and anti-capitalist, environmentalist —

A. LORENTZEN: Feminist.

GREIF: — feminist, thank you — feminist, progressive culture?

CLAYTON: And this when our discussion is taking place at the New School, where all those students were arrested yesterday for protesting, occupying 65 Fifth Avenue, right?

AUDIENCE MEMBER: One of the reasons it seems like the linkages aren't clear is that . . . What I liked about your talk is that you looked at the aesthetics of hipsterism, to try to understand it on its own terms. You tried to say, is there some deeper meaning to the particular signifiers of this movement? But maybe take a step back, and just start with the presumption that it's just random — like, it's just a group of people that chose a couple of common elements that they could use to create an in-group language, right? If that's the case, then grasping for these other linkages, it — it underscores why it doesn't make sense, because there isn't actually a politics to it, it's just a community of people who are in the same place.

One thing I want to throw out there is, if this is your reading, here's some weak evidence in support of it. We have to remember other things that are happening in America generally at this time. I can't really document this, all I can say is that I saw it happen in my family: middle of the country, by the 1970s and '80s, people lose their white ethnicity, it just gets obliterated. Betty Crocker cookbooks everywhere, right? It's just processed American stuff. But then in the '90s, especially in the early 2000s, you get this revival of what your grandparents were. Like, "My grandparents came here, and I'm Irish, and I have Irish stuff in my window and on my car." And I can't prove that those things didn't exist before I was alive, but I really don't think anyone embraced their inner Irishness until a certain point in the mid-'90s.

If your reading is a purely structural one — people looking for a language that bands them together as something, right? — then maybe the particular signifiers don't matter.

MICHELLE ANGEL MARTINEZ: I'm curious what you guys think about the child as hipster accessory.

Since we've talked so much about the innate desire of hipsters to be childlike or maintain a certain naiveté, I'm wondering about the hipsters who now have children, and strollers developed by NASA, and them bringing them to shows and to bars — how the child plays into continuing to develop as a hipster into later life.

C. LORENTZEN: You're talking about the critique that says that these people have children and then sort of use their children as conspicuous displays of their own taste, right? I mean, that's valid, that happens all the time.

It's disgusting. Totally revolting. It's really annoying when they bring their kids to parties and expect you to like their kids as much as you like their dogs. It works against having a good time, but it's one of the things that make people feel better about themselves, like they're a real person.

It reminds of — Mark had pointed to this sort of horse that gets beaten a lot in *n+1* discourse, which was Eggers and *McSweeney's* — but if you look at the first issue of *McSweeney's*, it says "This one's for the children." And in that context it's obviously a joke, but then a few years later all the people associated with *McSweeney's* — or a lot of them, probably — start having children, and they set up a charitable organization called 826, which certainly does a lot of good work, I'm not going to deny that . . . but one time I was walking down the street with a friend of mine who, granted, is now just a successful novelist who lives in France, but at the time he was volunteering or he had gotten some kind of grant and was working on literacy issues in Harlem, and we were walking by 826 in Park Slope and he's like, "Yeah, go set up your, you know, tutor center in the whitest neighborhood in town, that's going to do a lot of good."

This I think also relates to the issue of, "are hipsters progressive?" Whenever I see sort of conspicuous progressivism or conspicuous do-gooderism among hipsters, my first, instinctual reaction is suspicion.

A. LORENTZEN: I'd just like to make one clarification on Christian's point, where —

C. LORENTZEN: [*To the audience*] — She's my sister.

A. LORENTZEN: — If you read *A Heartbreaking Work*, Dave Eggers essentially already had a child, he had his younger brother, who he was raising —

C. LORENTZEN: Right, I'm not disputing that —

A. LORENTZEN: Can I speak! Whether or not *McSweeney's* issue one was a joke — maybe the rest of the *McSweeney's* crew started having babies, but he had a child from the beginning.

AUDIENCE MEMBER: But nothing with them was ever just like a joke. It was always playing both ways.

C. LORENTZEN: Yeah. Sure.

AUDIENCE MEMBER: Like the faux sincerity was never really faux.

C. LORENTZEN: Alright, but then later on you have the "child of the issue" in *The Believer* . . . I mean I don't think this is a controversial point I'm making.

CHARLES PETERSEN: I'm so glad we could have Christian here so we could have an example of a hipster. And I think that one thing —

C. LORENTZEN: A second-rate hipster. I think in your book [*speaking to Robert Lanham*] I would be a "pol-lit."

A. LORENTZEN: What does that mean?

LANHAM: It's a hipster that's obsessed with politics and literature and academia. Generally has a beard.

C. LORENTZEN: [*Strokes his beard*] In the picture in your book I think he has longer hair but I've unfortunately started to go bald.

PETERSEN: I'd like to present an alternative narrative of the hipster. I think one problem is that this discussion is premised on the death of the hipster, which "happened" in 2003, and I just think that the hipster is continually dying and being reborn. This is kind of a superficially Trotskyist view of the hipster as a continual revolution.

    I think that basically, when I think back to when I first heard of hipsters — because I'm from the middle of nowhere — it was in 2003 or 2002, when I first started reading Pitchfork, and at the time it seemed like such a great phenomenon. They were reacting against emo, which was the one thing in the world that needed to be destroyed in 2003, or against twee music, all these things that I really didn't like. So the first time that I heard something like *Losing My Edge*, which I think of as the ultimate hipster moment of the early part of this decade, it seemed great. And I think something like — um, I was 7 in 1991 — but I think that *Slanted and Enchanted* had roughly the same effect. I think that in 1966, '67, the Velvet Underground had a very similar effect. The hipsters are constantly destroying things. And we've been talking about "hipsterism" in this very broad way, which is how, say, *New York* magazine is using it right now, which I don't think is how we should be using it. It seems to me so many people who are described now as hipsters are clearly not hip; the thing about the hipster, as Mark said, is it's this — I forget which of the definitions it was, I think it was 3 — this *a priori* sense of absolute unimpeachable hipness . . . which I think we saw when Christian gave his speech. It was something that you cannot stand up against.

C. LORENTZEN: Don't try to.

PETERSEN: So at the moment that we're pronouncing the death of the hipster, that in itself is somewhat of a hipster moment. I think it goes along with what we were saying earlier about *n+1* being accused of being a hipster magazine, which is true, but not in the sense that "hipster" has come to mean now. It's hipster because it's destroying the current moment, in the same way that hipsters were hipsters because they were destroying things in 2003 and in 1991. I think that we were asking, why does this specific term "hipster" happen in 1999? Why do we go back to the 1950s, 1940s? I think the vast of majority of people who were using it in 2001, 1999 had no idea of any of those connotations. By that time it had been completely deracinated, and had just become a word with no history. And if you look at the word "hipster," it just simply means the hippest person in the room — the person who you can't stand up to. So I guess I just think that all this discussion has been useful in the sense of, "What is the massive subculture of youth today?" which is something that needs to be discussed — or, "What is our place as gentrifiers?" But these are all other discussions.

The question of the hipster is specifically one of, how do you accomplish revolution within subculture? I think that people keep saying, "Well, there are all these negative sides to the fact that there are subcultures, there are all these positive sides to the fact that there are subcultures." I think that in New York it's heightened because living within a subculture here you're much more intertwined with capitalism. If you live in Minneapolis, if you live even in a place like Seattle, you can still live ten minutes out of downtown for $300 a month. I mean, in New York it's absurd. I think this reveals a certain amount of provincialism in the discussion, because bohemianism in the rest of the country, at least in most of the rest of the country, is still really easy. You don't even have to work that hard. You don't have to have bedbugs. Bedbugs are a very New York phenomenon. You don't hear about them in other places. You can live on nothing. And I think that's also true in much of the rest of the world. In Western Europe, you have to live in Berlin — but there is at least somewhere to go.

So when talking about the hipster, I think that it's useful to ask, what's the best way to destroy things in order to produce new things? Which I think, if you look at something like — I mean the odd thing about Pavement is that there's *Slanted and Enchanted,* which is to me a completely destructive album that I love, and then you have *Crooked Rain, Crooked Rain* two or three years later, and to my mind they become a completely different band that I still really like — by turning things down, they actually produce something good. So I think in the same way that when you talk about revolution you need to ask how do you destroy things and yet start over.

GREIF: It would not be the worst thing if everyone were to come out of here having found that "the hipster" and "hipsterism" had lost its magic and we were no longer in thrall to this piece of terminology, which I certainly use, and I think many of us use, to pick people out.

I had anticipated a defense of the West Coast from Charles's remarks, because as far as New York–centric things go, certainly if you start looking at the creative material — "Definition #2" of the hipster, the hipster artist — often it seems hipster artists are not centered in New York at all. In fact, New York has had a pretty lousy track record, especially when it comes to music . . . but in California —

CORWYN LIGHT-WILLIAMS: Well, there was hip-hop.

GREIF: I mean just hipster music.

PETERSEN: Or Olympia, Washington, or Portland.

GREIF: Or Olympia, or Portland, or Seattle, San Francisco, et cetera.

LIGHT-WILLIAMS: All those people moved there from other places anyway, so I think it's kind of pointless to evaluate tax regions for their creative value.

GREIF: Pavement didn't move to Stockton, did they?

LIGHT-WILLIAMS: They're from Stockton, but they didn't record *Slanted and Enchanted* in Stockton because it was Stockton, but because someone's garage was there.

C. LORENTZEN: Well, certain of them had gone to UVA, and then they spent some time in New York and then they went back to California. I think Stephen Malkmus once remarked that they had actually sold out with *Slanted and Enchanted*, which was a betrayal of their earlier singles.

GREIF: I just wonder does someone — is there someone from the West Coast who wishes to speak for the West Coast and declare that in fact the hipster culture of the West Coast is different, significantly?

LIGHT-WILLIAMS: I'm actually from Portland, I'm visiting this weekend, and I have a friend who refers to Portland as the spiritual home of white men with glasses. So I think it's really interesting for me to be here and hear a very New York-centric — to my mind at least — point of view.

It's not the case that you can — I just want to clarify — get an apartment for $300 ten minutes from downtown Seattle.

PETERSEN: In the Central District, you can. I've lived there.

LIGHT-WILLIAMS: Kind of, but then you have bedbugs so maybe it's the same thing.

I want to say, I guess I've also been around the world and seen a lot of places that are just hipster-proof. And I think it was Jace who said you get a false positive going to some of these places, and I think that there is a really different culture on the West Coast because everything is smaller.

A lot of people go to Portland because it's sort of like the opposite of New York — where people say if you make it there you can make it anywhere — but Portland is like, if you didn't make it anywhere else, then you move to Portland. But I think that's why a lot of people are successful from a place like Portland; you can be a really big fish in a small pond and start succeeding and start getting traction, whereas if I were a musician and wanted to come to New York, I have no idea what I would do. I guess you could try desperately to play shows. But in Portland you can pretty quickly start getting into the big venues.

So I think that's the reason things come out of — I also lived in Olympia, Washington, for a while, and Seattle, so I've kind of had the full range of West Coast hipster experiences. I've been to a lot of big cities, but I get here and it does seem so hipster, but it also seems so entrenched, and there isn't anything as entrenched in Portland or Seattle. Those places seem to change really rapidly. Portland is really a great place as a sort of metaphor, I guess — it has a really great restaurant scene, and the reason is no restaurant lasts more than three months. I kind of feel like music's the same way. Stuff gets popular and it's really popular with everyone for a brief period and then utterly dies, or gets really successful and comes to New York. I do think the West Coast is different, but is there a specific question that you want me to comment on or is this good enough?

GREIF: [*Noticing that two hours have elapsed*] I feel like we're getting to that point — this happens on every panel — where we're clearly reaching the fatigue point, which I never believe is necessarily a reason to stop, although it makes sense to, and politeness usually requires it. We do have refreshments. But the question is, do people want to keep going? How much time do we actually have?

A. LORENTZEN: Chad's telling us to cut it off. We should take maybe two more questions.

GREIF: People can certainly hang out. Over cookies or whatever we have for refreshments. Crack cocaine.

LANHAM: It seems like there's been a lot of discussion about the death of the hipster that peaked in 2003–2004. But I do recall, when I was researching and writing my book in 2000–2001, one of the recurring jokes I was starting to write about and that ended up in the book was that . . . there's always a sense of a little bit of self-loathing with hipsters. So one of the recurring jokes in the book is any time I ask someone if they're a hipster, immediately the answer is "no." And I think we're continuing to see that, because I constantly hear that the hipster is a late '90s, early turn-of-the-century phenomenon, but then I turn on the television and I see *Flight of the Conchords*, which seems to me to have the kind of quintessential hipster aesthetic, hipster humor, hipster irony. Demetri Martin's another example, it seems. Sufjan Stevens, if you want to talk about the music world — you know, his back-up band dresses like Girl Scouts. And just looking around the room I could point out that this person looks like a hipster, this person looks like a hipster, you know, the dress is still there, the accoutrements. I think the ironic sensibility hasn't really faded. So I guess my question is, has the death arrived? I mean certainly there's backlash, and I think the backlash has grown, but if anything it seems to be thriving still.

C. LORENTZEN: I think it's funny — obviously television and the mainstream mass culture are always sort of behind the game, so I think you're right that a lot of that stuff has broken through. A lot of those guys, especially Demetri and the *Flight of the Conchords* people . . . and you start seeing villains in Batman movies that look like hipsters and you're like "whoa." Yeah. But I think that one thing that's happened, and you might be able to speak to this as well as I can, is that people have stopped calling me up and asking me to write articles with the H-word in it. Although there was that "hipster hookers" piece that came out in *Radar* toward the end, and it was funny because the author of that piece had started pitching me, as an editor, and when it came out — she was the writer on it, she was just pitching me ideas — she said, "This wasn't supposed to be about hipster hookers, they just put that word on it." It was just about, you know, young people who were hookers, in her mind.

But it sounds much better doesn't it, "hipster hookers"? I always thought of them as "hooksters." I think that we've reached a point of fatigue among us in New York in chattering about it, you know. Which maybe started with your book party at the Knitting Factory, which I snuck into, and then went on to hipster hookers. One cycle of magazine articles is over, but now we have TV shows and bestselling records.

LANHAM: I think the backlash is there, and there is hipster fatigue. But I guess the argument I'm trying to make is, if the hipster has died, what has replaced it? I think perhaps we are on the cusp of something else, but for all intents and purposes it seems like what I was satirizing in my book in the first place was that the first tenet of being a hipster is you deny being a hipster. I think there's a fatigue but it's just a perpetuation of the denial of being a hipster in the first place that I was satirizing in the book.

GREIF: I do want to clarify that rather than argue for the death of the hipster *per se*, I want to argue for a hipster Stage 1, and a hipster Stage 2 . . . like a rocket. It continues to change. Because we have this problem now of the hipster as global brand, right? Peruvian hipster haters, and Peruvian hipsters.

Are there structural things which would give a kind of long-term global life to the hipster? Jace, can you imagine that five years from now you could show up to play somewhere overseas, and *everyone* would be wearing skinny jeans?

CLAYTON: I think a lot of it has to do with just fashions synchronizing faster because of all the internet gossip sites — Facebook, Myspace, all this — so that people can see what the cool kids are doing in other cities. And kids are traveling more between cities. I mean, not in Peru — but there's a much greater awareness which is only going to continue as the internet goes deeper and deeper, so suddenly you'll get Moroccan hipsters and so on and so forth. I think there are a lot of tunnels and bridges toward a specific level of sameness.

GREIF: You think it's still coming from the metropole.

CLAYTON: I think it's still coming from the metropole, but no longer New York — this New York-centricity is kind of fading away, some of it, so as soon as the Austrian kids get their cameras on, they'll be blasting images of their parties . . . In terms of talking about the "global hipster" as a brand. The thing is, companies latch onto that, as soon as there's a subculture they say, "Hey, we can market that," which just reinforces it.

KYLE STURGEON: I have a minor hypothesis about one branch of the future hipster, based on some observations I've made, coming from Louisville, Kentucky to New York recently. This can incorporate some of what Jace and Mark have said. Mark, your third definition of the hipster I think incorporates what William Gibson calls "pattern recognition," which is the ability to spot trends. I think one of those trends has been the hipster's new political philosopher: Slavoj Žižek. And I think Jace could sponsor this, because I know that one of the biggest *cumbia* clubs is called Žižek. And so it's funny, when you talk about the political future of the hipster, if you actually follow the precepts of Žižek — who tells you to do nothing in the face of economic tragedy, so on and so forth — it seems like maybe one reason why pattern recognition led to Žižek is because of the way he treats contemporary media and the films that he has, but also because he tells you literally: "Don't do anything. You don't have to do anything." It's like the opposite of Rorty's campaign: "There's nothing to do."

But I think there's a danger for *n+1*. Recently, William Deresiewicz called you guys a hipster journal in the *Nation*. I wasn't all that surprised to read that, especially coming from him. But isn't there a danger, Mark, that *n+1* . . . My inclination, my guess, would be that most of the editors at *n+1* don't care too much for Slavoj Žižek, that's just a guess. But isn't there a danger that — as hipsters co-opt this weird Marxism or post-Marxism — that you will be misidentified with this political philosophy which says do nothing, which I think is not what you want people to do? And maybe that's why you were called a hipster journal. That's a question.

JAMES POGUE: Very quickly: I think that speaks to something, but if you want to look at political activism *à la* the hipster as it has developed especially in New York and San Francisco, it's much closer to what you're talking about with Crimethinc, where a lot of these people grew up reading that, and reading Akhasic Books and stuff, and they're not hitchhiking anymore, but they're dropping out. And I don't think it's a very Žižekian "do nothing," it's: "be an activist by not participating." I think that is, to a certain extent, one of the things that's harder to criticize about the hipster than others. I think that it's produced some positive things, as easy to make fun of them as they are.

STURGEON: I just met a thousand Žižekians at Barnes and Noble, where they were all buying his book.

TKACIK: I used to work at American Apparel and he was seriously the only intellectual that any of them had heard of.

POGUE: Do you have the sense that, inasmuch as we're arguing. . . I just feel like hipsters are denuded of political impulses.

STURGEON: They're not! Like *cumbia* — like the biggest club of one of the biggest new music styles coming out — a global phenomenon — the club is called Žižek.

POGUE: I know, but what does that matter?

STURGEON: That's my point. It's completely vacuous. They're adopting a political philosophy that is empty.

C. LORENTZEN: I don't think they know what the political philosophy really is.

POGUE: That's what *I'm* saying —

C. LORENTZEN: I mean Žižek is a celebrity with a look to him, and his most popular writings are his movie criticism. I mean, I don't think that —

STURGEON: I agree with you. But let me further my point. So, as in Charles Petersen's Trotskyist scheme, one of the things that happens with media outlets is that they get really, really popular, usually for a bad reason, and then everybody stops reading them. I guess my question is directly about the health of *n+1*. I was asking a really specific question of Mark. I'm not saying that these people actually *read* Žižek. I'm saying, isn't there a danger that a whole lot of people are about to start "reading" your magazine — just because of Žižek? Isn't this the symptom of a larger problem?

GREIF: Wow. Um. Is there a danger that enormous numbers of people will begin reading *n+1*? Um. Well, I fear that there is.

[Audience laughter]

I think your original question seemed to be tilting toward a worry about do-nothingism. I don't think Žižek will be remembered in fifty years. I don't view him as a problem.

C. LORENTZEN: I have another question, though, along the same lines. One criticism I heard voiced about *n+1* during the last year by some young writers, even ex-interns of *n+1*, was that *n+1* was not doing enough to defeat the Republicans in the election.

GREIF: I do think that, constitutionally and temperamentally, there is something about the editorial staff of *n+1* which is occasionally afflicted with do-nothingism.

But this seems — as far as it speaks to the future — to speak to the question of whether in fact we are positioned to "do" something, or do anything. This certainly seems like the right moment after the election to ask. We'll have to see.

But what are we going to do? Because, really — fatigue has set in. I can see it in everyone's posture. And yet there are important questions waiting at the microphones. Should we get some cookies, or whatever? I don't know why I keep saying cookies. It's infantilizing. It's clearly what I want.

C. LORENTZEN: I would like a cigarette.

GREIF: Should we at least take a break? People can just come up, and we'll talk without the microphones?

[*Conversation continued informally in the lobby*]

DOSSIER

THE DEATH OF THE HIPSTER

*Originally published in "Marginal Utility,"
PopMatters.com. April 13, 2009.*

I WENT TO *n+1*'s "What Was the Hipster?" panel discussion at the New School on Saturday but went away a bit unfulfilled. There was little evidence presented that hipsterism is over — or that it was a concrete product of a specific historic moment — and no coherent theories for what might supplant it. The participants never really made much of an effort to establish a stable definition of what a hipster is, despite *n+1* editor Mark Greif's valiant effort in his opening remarks. He wondered if the white-trash-worshipping 1999 model of the hipster (the one that wore trucker hats, listened to redneck music, and oozed an aesthetic derived from a largely hypothetical and imaginatively reconstructed 1970s rec-room amateur porn) was the hipster qua hipster, the only one deserving of the title, the way those from the late 1950s and early 1960s who fit the Maynard G. Krebs caricature were the only actual beatniks, and the San Francisco arrivistes in 1967 were the only true hippies.

Or is the hipster a kind of permanent cultural middleman in hyper-mediated late capitalism, selling out alternative sources of social power developed by outsider groups — just as the original "White Negroes" evoked by Norman Mailer did to the original, pre-pejorative "hipsters," blacks looking for modes of social expression that could serve as a source of pride, power, and unification, and as emblems of resistance? Hipsters are the infiltrators who spoil the resistance, the cool-hunting collaborators and spies.

This struck me as a really interesting question: Are outsider groups the only ones that make possible new forms of cultural capital? And thus are hipsters always necessary to the powers that be? Perhaps, in an endlessly repeating pattern of co-optation, hipsters serve as agents for the stakeholders in the established cultural hegemony, appropriating the new cultural capital forms, delivering them to mainstream media in a commercial form and stripping their inventors' groups (if not the inventors themselves, in the best-case scenario) of the power and the glory, the unification and the mode of resistance.

As Greif mentioned in his talk, hipsters function as a "poison" conduit between the marketing machine and the street. Does the internet jeopardize this cozy relation between power groups and their hipster minions, or does it assure that the circuit will always be completed, forcing resistance further underground, perhaps into a region where it cannot be expressed publicly in any form without always already being co-opted? (Can you perform a significant act of rebellion on Facebook?) Jace Clayton, another of the panel speakers, discussed how the internet seemed to foster a globalized hipster brand that obviated organic local scenes or made them seem passé. As I understood it, his point was that the internet has made international recognition the standard of relevance for cultures that once were detached from and unrecognized by Anglo-American media. Those who revel in and facilitate that recognition are the hipsters of places like Peru.

I was all ready for a more thorough exploration of the ideas the panelists opened with, but that conversation never materialized. The sputtering confusion of the group discussion at the panel may have been inevitable. It's impossible to obtain objective distance from hipsterism; if you are concerned enough about the phenomenon to analyze it and discuss it, you are already somewhere on the continuum of hipsterism and are in the process of trying to rid yourself of its "taint" — as *n+1*'s announcement of the event noted.

We all had a stake in defining "hipster" as "not me." I thought that would be the core of the discussion, the paradoxes of that apparent truth. In always pushing ourselves to repudiate hipsterism, we may drive ourselves to new ways to conceive of our identity — but what good are these if they're always ripe for becoming the new modes of hipsterdom? What good is it to stay a few steps ahead if you always remain on the hipster path? How do we stop running that race, stop worrying about the degree to which we are "hip," the degree to which our treasured self-conceptions can be made into clichés against our will?

The problem with hipsters seems to me the way in which they reduce the particularity of anything you might be curious about or invested in into the same dreary common denominator of how "cool" it is perceived to be. Everything becomes just another signifier of personal identity. Thus hipsterism forces on us a sense of the burden of identity, of constantly having to curate it if only to avoid seeming like a hipster. But are there hipsters, actual hipsters, or just a pervasive fear of hipsters? Hipster hatred may actually precede hipsters themselves. Maybe that collective fear and contempt conjures them into being, just as the Red Scare saw communists everywhere, or how the Stasi made spies of everyone. Late capitalism makes us all fear being a hipster and thus makes us all into one, to some degree.

The hipster, then, is the bogeyman who keeps us from becoming too settled in our identity, keeps us moving forward into new fashions, keep us consuming more "creatively" and discovering new things that haven't become lame and hipster. We keep consuming more, and more cravenly, yet this always seems to us to be the hipster's fault, not our own.

One must start with the premise that the hipster is defined by a lack of authenticity, by a sense of lateness to the scene, or by the fact that his arrival fashions the scene — transforms people who are doing their thing into a self-conscious scene, something others can scrutinize and exploit. The hipster is that person who shows up and seems to ruin things — then you can begin to ask why this person exists, whether he is inevitable, whether he can be stopped, and what it will take. The hipster's presence specifically forms the illusion of inside and outside, and the idea that others will pay for the privilege of being shown through the gate.

The audience didn't regard the quest for a stable position from which to critique hipsterism as a challenge; ignoring it, it did not rise above postures of self-defense and projection. Instead, when audience members began to contribute to the discussion, it began to feel factional and accusatory, as if many had gathered to accuse everyone else of being hipsters, or at least to mock *n+1* itself for presuming it had somehow escaped hipsterism and insult its editors to their faces and show them what pretentious hipsters they themselves are. They seemed to want to peg *n+1* as a hipster vehicle, as failing to escape the trap it sometimes seems to wish to spring on others. One audience member asked the *n+1* editor if he was afraid the magazine would get too many readers, because presumably there are some readers who shouldn't be allowed to subscribe, who would tarnish the brand. Somewhat inexplicably, these "wrong" sort of readers were associated in the questioner's mind with Slavoj Žižek, his trendiness among philosophical name-droppers, and his alleged nihilism. Perhaps his question was whether *n+1* feared becoming trendy and then thereby vulnerable to the nonsensical and non-comprehending attacks and dismissals that Žižek himself is subjected to by the likes of this questioner.

The faint air of self-satisfaction inherent in the premise of a post-hipster conference grew thicker and thicker, and the tacit and necessary agreement to use terminology in the same way to move forward was increasingly ignored. Some even seemed to confuse hipsterism with an artistic avant-garde when they are in fact opposites by definition (by my definition anyway, and by any that would make the hipster a discrete object of analysis).

There was some discussion of the hipster as the embodiment of postmodernism as a spent force, revealing what happens when pastiche and irony exhaust themselves as aesthetics. But one could hear mutterings in the crowd that no one had the right to judge what cultural products were better than others, and it was clear that this audience was not ready to surrender cultural relativism and subjectivism, that they still wanted to remain mired in that endless fight. (Statement actually overheard in the lecture hall: "What gives you the right to say that *Charles in Charge* is not important!") The tenor of the discussion made me wonder if *n+1* wouldn't eventually take a *New Criterion* turn in its future and try to escape hipsterism and pop-tart relativism by hewing to a conservative ethic. I hope not, but it seems latent in the air of arrogant fustiness it sometimes projects. The more its would-be audience reviles it for its unrepentant intellectualism, the more it may steer toward a weary elitism.

HIPSTERS DIE ANOTHER DEATH AT *n+1* PANEL

'People Called Hipsters Just Happened to Be Young, and, More Often Than Not, Funny-Looking'

Originally published in the New York Observer.
April 13, 2009.

" **I** AM NOT NOW, nor have I ever been, a hipster," vowed *Harper's* senior editor Christian Lorentzen at a panel discussion provocatively titled "What Was the Hipster?," organized by *n+1*, and held at the New School on Saturday afternoon.

Despite L train maintenance and the kind of steady rain that can wreck perfectly asymmetrical bangs (not to mention a recent attempted occupation by students), about 100 attendees packed the Eugene Lang Center for a ridiculously wide-ranging discussion of hipster culture, which included heady thoughts on postcolonialism, deregulation, easy credit, Chinese ownership of US debt, Leon Trotsky, Slavoj Žižek, Pavement, Nirvana, Debbie Gibson, and Scott Baio.

It was one of those kinds of events.

Mr. Lorentzen, who penned a polemic called "Why The Hipster Must Die" for *Time Out New York* in 2007, declared the idea of the hipster a great fraud, and said he had come to apologize for his part in it. "No member of my family, no close friend, no enemy, no rival, no dance partner, no party guest, no barkeep, no doctor, no lawyer, no banker, no artist, no guitar player, no deejay, no model, no photographer, no author, no pilot, no stewardess, no actor, no actress, no television personality, no robber, no cop, no priest, no nun, no hooker, no pimp, no acquaintance known to me, has ever been a hipster," Mr. Lorentzen said.

"The fraud held that there are people called hipsters who follow a creed called hipsterism and exist in a realm called hipsterdom," he continued. "The truth is that there was no such culture worth speaking of, and the people called hipsters just happened to be young, and, more often than not, funny-looking."

Mr. Lorentzen, dressed in a black suit, seemed to be the only one poking fun at the topic. *n+1* editor and Eugene Lang assistant professor Mark Greif (grayish suit) offered a more academic talk, positing three definitions of the hipster, post-1999 — which the panel seemed to agree was the year the neo-hipster was born. (No matter that by 2004, *New York* magazine was already declaring the end of them all in a satire by Zev Borow.)

There were some uncomfortable moments: the one guy sporting a trucker hat stared straight ahead as Mr. Greif talked about how guys in trucker hats were striving for some sort of faux-authenticity. And when Mr. Greif hit upon the prevalence of pornographic and pedophilic mustaches among hipsters, one heavily mustachioed man seemed to listen more intently, while his thinly 'stached friend mustered an awkward laugh.

Jace Clayton (black jacket, black T-shirt, and faded black pants), a.k.a. DJ /rupture, wrapped up the panel portion by saying that artists, not hipsters, are "gentrification's shock troops," and that the hipster was just a "straw man in tight jeans."

"I imagine that folks moving to Bushwick open their closet and find no tube socks and think, 'I'm not a hipster, my parents don't pay my rent, I listen to classic country music without a trace of irony,' and then go on being the same arrogant, overprivileged people with the smug satisfaction that it's only hipsters who destroy neighborhoods, not them or their friends."

During the question and answer portion, several people wondered whether hipsters were intellectuals beneath their fashionable get-ups. "I would dispute that at the core of hipsterism is intellectualism," Mr. Lorentzen said.

"I say this based on my living in Williamsburg for two years. In Williamsburg, where everyone looked like that, a lot of people didn't know a damn thing."

The moderator, who happened to be Mr. Lorentzen's sister, Allison, challenged him on that: "Can you name the other places where you lived where people were well-read?"

"Park Slope, Windsor Terrace, Fort Greene, Clinton Hill, Cambridge, Somerville," he replied. "Not necessarily Hopkinton, Massachusetts." (Mr. Lorentzen has written about at least one of these neighborhoods before.)

Later, there was a discussion about Mr. Žižek, who apparently stands as the Father of Modern Hipster Thought. "I used to work at American Apparel, and he was the only intellectual anyone had heard of," a woman chimed in from the crowd. (Maybe it's Professor Žižek's shared affinities with American Apparel founder Dov Charney?)

Another woman asked about nostalgia (which felt, indeed, like a nostalgic question). "Do you guys think nostalgia is the right term for it? To me that sort of implies that we would have stopped talking about

Charles In Charge, but I'm not sure that that conversation ever stopped," she said.

"Why would nostalgia make you stop talking about *Charles In Charge*?" Mr. Greif wondered, which seemed to flummox the questioner.

One young man in wire-frame glasses and a green flannel over a button-up shirt bravely admitted to liking the idea of hipsterism when he read about it on Pitchfork in 2002 or 2003.

"The moment we're pronouncing the death of the hipster is, in itself, something of a hipster moment," he said.

"I think we in New York have just reached a point of fatigue in talking about it," proclaimed Mr. Lorentzen.

"People have stopped calling me up and asking me to write articles with the h-word in it."

RESPONSES

WILLIAMSBURG YEAR ZERO

MY SON AND I used to live in Williamsburg, Brooklyn. He was once in his stroller on Bedford Avenue when a twentysomething guy emerged from his apartment on North 8th Street decked out in full hipster uniform. He was as skinny as *OC*-era Mischa Barton, with miniscule black pegged jeans, a black T-shirt, dyed black hair, and a wide-brim, black hat of the sort Zorro might wear. My son gazed at him and said in the voice of the unselfconscious toddler, "Look at that old witch!" The guy, young and self-conscious, appeared humiliated.

I love this story. I don't know exactly what causes my knee to jerk toward contempt when I speak of "hipsters" or pass these young, interestingly dressed people on the street, but I'm not alone. Not only would no one ever admit to being a hipster — it's like claiming to be a JAP — it's remarkable how attuned New York peers of mine are to the offensiveness of the skinny-jeans set. Take Andrew, a lawyer friend of mine in his late twenties who wears skater clothes in his private time, though he isn't a skater. He leapt off the couch when I said I was writing about hipsters and regaled me with his opinions, all negative. The next day he sent me more thoughts. "At the risk of sounding like my grandfather (and father, for that matter), one problem I have with those damn kids is that a prime attribute of their character is to be a snob or to be pretentious," wrote Andrew. He continued:

> And yet, they don't really create anything themselves. In this way, they are kind of like critics. Overall, their culture is that of the 21st-century slacker. I realize that this is a stereotype; I'm sure there are plenty of doctors, USAID workers and salt-of-the-earth types that have bushy mustaches, wear skinny plaid pants and showcase "I Eat Bush" t-shirts (in a cursive font, of course).

Andrew hates hipsters' inauthenticity, he says, and defends his own adoption of skater regalia as an homage to a culture that is authentic. "I like the skater vibe because, while 'skater' used to be synonymous with 'slacker,' I don't think that is true anymore. Now skaters are known as fearless extremists (like the

Jackass guys). For the record, I am scared of my own shadow, so this character trait does not apply to me."

To me, Andrew's logic is contradictory. He hates that hipsters are hangers-on or snide critics alongside cultures of creators — real artists, musicians, and writers (the type who deserve to wear skinny jeans or ironic facial hair, I wonder?). But he is protective of his own desire to look like a skater, even though he doesn't skate and isn't particularly bold (the attribute of skaters that he admires). The distinction he appears to be making is that he loves skaters, whereas hipsters are too cynical and self-conscious to love a creative culture and imitate it.

Those who sneer at hipsters often belong to the hipster's social class. Using myself as an example, I was a gentrifier in Williamsburg. Like the maligned hipsters, I used my parents' savings to secure a place to live. While I was a single mother who lived check to check, and while I often woke up at night worrying about how I was going to pay the bills, I probably had more in common with the college-educated white hipsters in my neighborhood than with the working single moms, Polish and Latina, who were the long-time residents of my stretch of Brooklyn. I wanted grocery stores that carried organic products like Horizon milk for $6 per half-gallon, and overpriced but aesthetically satisfying coffee shops like El Beit. I needed expensive boutiques, otherwise I would have felt bad for having

left Manhattan. I loved Bedford Cheese and Marlow &
Sons and the extensive and rarefied selection of beers
at Spuyten Duyvil. I hoped for property values to rise,
so that I could sell my apartment for a profit.

Hipster hating speaks to our own fears and inad-
equacies more than it says anything real about real
people. It's like the hatred Martha Stewart provoked
for showing women that you could make domesticity
into an art *and* a multimillion dollar fortune, or the
contempt many have felt for Hillary Clinton for prov-
ing that you could be more ambitious than most men
and still be a mother. Hipsters remind us of . . . I don't
know — youth and daring and style, that we don't have
anymore or perhaps never did?

The critique of their physical appearance also
makes me wonder about the gender of hipsters. They
are feminized (skinny, fashion-y, coiffed) but they
are also — to judge from the figures name-checked
as hipsters during the panel — mostly men. Is there
homophobia in the hipster-hating, a revulsion in seeing
men who care "too much" about how they look? Is my
own irritation due in part to the fact that hipsterism is
male-dominated, just as *n+1* is?

I MOVED OUT of Williamsburg. I now live in
Greenwich Village, which is fusty and wealthy,
but was once the province of bohemia. At 40, I'm
young for my neighborhood, and it's a relief not to be

reminded every day of how old I'm getting. When I visit my old neighborhood, I smile at the leg warmers on the girls, the Sally Jesse Raphael glasses and thin asslessness of the men. I wonder what they see when they look at me. I pray no one says under his or her breath, "Look at that old witch."

19 QUESTIONS

I BECAME A TEENAGER in 1960. I spent my high school years admiring and trying to emulate the creeds and tastes of '40s and '50s hipsters — and then, after 1964, moved along with them as these creeds and tastes modulated and diversified through the Civil Rights and youth movements, the counterculture, the New Left, and Black Power, feminism, and gay rights.

I can't pretend to know much firsthand about the new hipsters of the last decade. It interests me that "hip-hop" also gestured to similar origins when it took the "hip" from "hipster." Can it be a cultural accident that within about twenty years of each other, black and white vanguardists (and arrivistes) drew on the old black and white uses of the same word? And then further segregated its meanings via their musical, social, and style codes?

Clearly, the first hipsters craved racial variety when it came to tastes and icons. There was plenty of tension and competition, but the need was evident — and not just in Norman Mailer's exorbitant "White Negro" proclamations. Music provides the best example. In jazz you had a spectrum from Miles Davis to Chet Baker of musicians who seemed distinct, but not segregated. Davis's *Birth of the Cool* sessions defined a common aesthetic of black and white musicians that linked New York bop to the West Coast cool school. But in the literary and stage arts one could also cite the alliance of LeRoi and Hettie Jones, and the indeterminacy or intermediateness of Anatole Broyard, and the variety of the Off-Broadway scene. Is the recent hipster world really as racially singular as the music and films and books named in the transcript indicate? Is that possible?

In many ways popular music does now seem as segregated as it often appeared in the '40s and '50s. The difference? Today it looks like the result of cultural choice and niche constituencies rather than entrenched race politics and economics. Clearly there are simply many more sub- and sub-subcultures of music to choose from these days, all of them with style markers that matter — markers that are socio-economic and cultural, decipherable by any high-school kid, and reinforced by the iron discipline of teasing and disparagement. How do neighborhood makeup and gentrification — with their strains (but also juxtapositions) of classes, races, ethnicities — mark hipster tastes and determine fetish objects? Aren't there significant nonwhite hipster tastes: keywords, emblems, bands, movies, clothes? Are there — or have there been, since the late 1990s — significant, clearly evident, and imitable nonwhite hipsters, and not just "exceptions"?

I WAS PARTICULARLY interested in the periodizing and analysis of a white ethnic or working-class aesthetic. Doesn't it seem as if that working-class Pittsburgh ethnic, Andy Warhol, born "Warhola," set us up for all of this irony about the trappings of mass-produced homogeneity in the early 1960s, with his Brillo boxes and soup cans? Surely he set us up for a way out, too — and that is also why I was surprised to see that the "white ethnic irony" question had been shorn of its own proper history.

This aesthetic had a surge in the late 1980s, in the Reagan years of highly unequal advancing wealth, framed by two recessions. At that time, the media tended to label it a "white trash" fad, naming the people who had been left behind in some dump of the American racial mind.

Some of the emblems and icons: plastic flowers, loud chunky costume jewelry. The trucker look, some trucker talk. Cajun and country western. Lots of old-school Southern redneck stuff; strenuously arch, often patronizing, while aiming for irony. "White trash" cookbooks and "white trash" guidebooks. Snarky movies like the Coen Brothers' *Raising Arizona* and David Byrne's *True Stories*. White ethnics showed up in quirkier, cleverer settings, where the aesthetic was often deliberately queer or complicatedly attached to "bad taste" and bids for freedom: John Waters movies, the clothes of Cyndi Lauper and Madonna, even the Boston Irish bar boys of *Cheers*. Italian ethnics got some irony and romantic comedy relief in *Moonstruck*. And Jonathan Demme had his cross-class and culture miscegenation movies, too, with *Something Wild* and *Melvin and Howard*. It was as if, with fears of Reagan's capitalism sinking the whole ship of democracy, people were seeking fantasies about a more generous and diverse life at the bottom, to keep them warm.

All this was also happening, too, as whiteness studies was taking hold in the academy, and stirring up some shit. The basic quarrel, still unresolved: was whiteness studies really a critique of white power structures and ideologies motivated by Afro-American studies? Or was it a cunning way to reclaim center stage in the university from the multi-cultural reorganization set in motion by programs of black, Chicano, Asian, women's and queer studies and cultures (no longer called "subcultures")? Is there a contemporary testing of intellectual disciplines on the horizon that will unsettle us again? I don't know.

There's something worrisome, after all, in the persistent return of Mommy, Daddy, and childhood dream days, which the panel revisited. How much does this preserving of the adult world one knew as a child really set the boundaries (unconsciously as much as consciously) of one's tastes and choices? I know this is a huge generalization, but that impulse truly did not characterize the '40s and '50s hipsters. They claimed — sometimes desperately, often clumsily, by no means always effectively — to be consciously separating themselves from the look, the sound, the artifacts, the sensory world of their parents as well as that social, political, and (sometimes) economic world.

Finally, look at this exchange: "Do we believe an attachment remains — a genuine attachment — between hipster culture and anti-capitalist, environmentalist . . ." "Feminist!" ". . . feminist, thank you — feminist, progressive culture?"

What I can't tell, and I hope this shows my ignorance, is how powerful as agents — as artists, as shapers — women are in contemporary hipster culture. Riot grrrls were mentioned. There are female musicians in some of the named bands. But what else? Where else? Who else? In the old days, we were artifacts, consumers, muses, and accessories. How about now? Are there dyke, fag, tranny icons and participants? I just can't tell if queer culture overlaps with hipster culture. But I would be depressed if it didn't.

HIP-HOP & HIPSTERISM

Notes on a Philosophy of Us & Them

There is a difference . . . between Norman and myself in that I think he still imagines that he has something to save, whereas I have never had anything to lose. Or, perhaps I ought to put it another way: the things that most white people imagine that they can salvage from the storm of life is really, in sum, their innocence. It was this commodity precisely which I had to get rid of at once, literally, on pain of death.

—James Baldwin

THE QUOTATION comes from James Baldwin's "love letter" to Norman Mailer, "The Black Boy Looks at the White Boy," published in *Esquire* four years after Mailer's "The White Negro" first appeared in *Dissent* in 1957. If the *n+1* panel is an update of

Mailer's attempt to define the hipster, then consider my response an update of Baldwin's dismissive, but gracious, riposte.

The hipster strikes me as an avatar of innocence. No one self-identifies as a hipster. Baldwin's point was to suggest that an essay on the White Negro — analogous, I'd argue, to a panel on hipsters — is the indulgence of a dream, a fantasy, that arises from the luxury of sleeping through life. (Nietzsche's first maxim in *Twilight of the Idols*: "Idleness is the beginning of all psychology.") And Baldwin's sentiment cuts right to the heart of what white privilege in America is about: the artful shirking of human responsibility in the face of ongoing injustice; a certain entitled pacifism that preserves the status quo of Us and Them. They say the issue of class is about the Haves and the Have Nots, but that's only a small remove from the conversation of Us and Them. And the hipster discussion, much like Mailer's "White Negro" essay, is a different kind of discussion: one about Us and Them, carried on almost entirely among those who Have.

AFTER RECEIVING THE transcript of the *n+1* panel, I talked about contemporary hipsters with: my father (55, black); two of my good guy friends (37 and 30, black); my girlfriend's mom (57, Puerto Rican); my girlfriend's dad (age indeterminate, Italian); my girlfriend's sister (thirtysomething, Itali-Rican), and a smattering of others who would fit under the rubric of "peers." No one apart from those who read my blog (often for reasons of personal loyalty) demonstrated any real familiarity with the term. Which is to say, besides with folks who might have gone to the panel, there wasn't a conversation to be had. No one was too taken with the concept after I spelled out the relevant details, either. "You mean young people?" was a common response. Glazed eyes was another.

I grew up in the South Bronx in the '80s, and in the mid-'90s was plucked from there and escorted to boarding school in pastoral Connecticut (Choate Rosemary Hall, Pomfret). In my years at school, and subsequently at college (Trinity, in Hartford), I never once heard the term "hipster." Looking back, I think hipsters, yuppies, and preppies were the same thing to a black person in my position. We didn't classify people beyond the fundamentals of race, money, and maybe social skills. A friend might have referred to what others would call a "hipster" as "rich white awkward dude," or maybe "white, rich, skinny-pants-wearing motherfucker, but he's cool though." I can't say that this doesn't feel — in my experience anyway — more semantically rich and more to the point. Which makes me think that the term "hipster" functions within a world of small distinctions where people don't want to name the facts, and that it has some sort of repressed white-American sensibility in its essence. (I remember reading *n+1*'s opening manifesto: "Say what you mean!")

IN 2010, in contemporary hip-hop culture, it's actually a bit of a surprise that there isn't much "hipster" talk thrown around. Drake used a line in his *So Far Gone* mixtape, "me doing shows getting everyone nervous, cause them hipsters gonna have to get along with them hood niggas" — but there "hipster" was just used to signify the artist's wide-ranging pop appeal. In the context of rapping, it's more an aesthetic flourish and boast than a substantive commentary. "These preppies gonna have to get along with these thugs" would have been the line a few years ago.

It's been used as an insult on occasion, certainly. The panel points out that one of the odd distinctions about the term "hipster" was that even at the peak of its significance, no group claimed it for itself. Well, if you thought hipsters didn't like hipsters, hip-hop *really* didn't like hipsters; the few times I heard of the label getting slung at people in the hip-hop community, the pejorative quality was only multiplied. In June 2008, *XXL* magazine published a piece re-examining so-called "Hipster Rap" and defending rappers who had been identified as hipsters for not exhibiting certain hip-hop tropes.* A true hipster rapper

---

* *XXL* Staff, "Hipster Boogie," *XXL*, June 2008.

would've been the epitome of an Uncle Tom, exploiting a robust, nourishing culture to create an empty white-friendly shell — which the alleged hipsters were not. So *XXL* created an acronym, SCHR (So-Called Hipster Rap) and defended rappers like The Cool Kids, Lupe Fiasco, The Knux, Kidz In The Hall, Kid Sister, and Wale from the accusation.

This list of acts updated a type of artist once slandered as "Backpack Rap" at the turn of the century: Mos Def, Talib Kweli, and The Roots — whose styles were distinguished from the pop-oriented emcees Jay-Z and 50 Cent. The "Backpack Rap" slander was itself a continuation of the hostility to the Native Tongue groups of the late '80s and early '90s, the era of A Tribe Called Quest, De La Soul, and the kindred Queen Latifah. The antagonism to these groups reflected the original "commercial" versus "conscious" dichotomy in the consumption of hip-hop culture that, of course, was false from the start — or too simplified, overly reductive. De La Soul's second album, *De La Soul Is Dead*, was a concept record responding to the accusation that De La Soul were "hippies." In hindsight, this feels like an early variation of the hipster criticism — at least in the context of hip-hop vernacular, where the taxonomies of white people are less nuanced. *De La Soul Is Dead* toys with the psychology and cyclical conceit of the question, "Are Hipsters Dead?"

THE VENOMOUS MONIKER "hipster rap" can be distinguished from another coinage I've been working on: the "Blipster," or black hipster. With the Blipster, we're talking more about personal fashion and individual hobby interests. After all, hipsters are allowed to be any ethnicity — you can be a white skinny-pants wearing person, or you can be a black skinny-pants wearing person. You might be mocked by friends, sure, as any weird clothing might get you mocked — but it's not as insidious a crime in the black community as being a hipster rapper. In my view, the Blipster is a contemporary update on the cool black nerd, picking stuff up from white sub-culture to develop an accepted type. These skinny, nappy-facial-haired black dudes might even be avatars of our ethnocultural future.

The outcome is a group like Ninjasonik that wears Blipster fashion and makes hip-hop/techno-punk music. They have a song called "Tight Pants," featuring a hook that goes: "I'm a tight-pants-wearing-ass nigga," over and over again, and a song using Tracy Morgan's infamous "Somebody's gonna get pregnant" line. Both suggest the hipster signifiers of irony, distance, and detachment are just starting to emerge for hip-hop artists who can actually embrace it. If hipsters represent some sort of cultural exhaustion, then Ninjasonik indicates that once black people have enough middle-class traction, a certain bourgeois comfort level, then, and only then, will the hipster bogeyman raise his head for them, too, as a sort of cultural scarecrow. In time, every culture gets its hipster.

And yet, this interpretation only sticks if we ignore the legacy of hip-hop, and the fundamental vein of irony and comedy it's kept close to its heart. Prince Paul, on his *Psychoanalysis: What Is It?* and his hip-hop opera *A Prince Among Thieves,* and De La Soul, on their *3 Feet High and Rising* and *De La Soul is Dead,* pretty much invented the "hip-hop sketch" as a form of urban avant-garde satire. Other quirky comic artists that predated the contemporary hip-hop explosion are Dana Dane ("Nightmares"), Biz Markie ("Pickin' Boogers"), Slick Rick ("Lick the Balls"), and another one you might have heard of, Will Smith, the first hip-hop Grammy award winner. These guys were storytellers, with self-conscious, even meta lyrics, always subversive of the tough-talk of so-called "gangsta rap" as well as the militant politics of so-called "conscious rap." There was a certain innocence in the consciousness of a lot of early hip-hop, an innocence that finds echoes in our vision of the hipster today.

A S A BLACK BOY looking at white boys, hipsterism strikes me as what happens when white folks become aware of power and inequity — but then say, "Well, what are we supposed to do? Throw our hands up and mug for the camera." Any relinquishing of power is inevitably an aesthetic gesture.

Young people who grew up during the hip-hop explosion saw it empower black people, but also saw it enter the same system of commercial exploitation that created preppies, yuppies, and all the rest. If hip-hop learned by watching white America, then maybe the new young white America said — in its best and only attempt to try and help correct things — "Look, we're going to make ourselves so silly, so pathetically empty, that you have to get back to the roots of what you believe and want, and in turn, help us get back to the roots of what we believe and want." And what we all want is to find the means of turning a philosophy of Us and Them into simply Us.

Hip-hop allows for the same conversation, one about Us and Them, but also steers toward more substance, content, real people, and real issues of inequity and injustice. I mean to say: if you're talking about hipsters and want to get somewhere, you might be better off just talking hip-hop. To more directly get to the point. To make your words and ideas more actionable. To skip indulging in intellectual exercises like the "White Negro," and go the more difficult route: learning hip-hop codes and sensibilities, because it's a culture, not a shell or an aesthetic. It has depth. If both hipsterism and hip-hop are doors to move all of us on to a shared place, hip-hop is the one that isn't revolving, returning you to where you started.

ESSAYS

ON DOUCHEBAGS

"Now that we've infiltrated the mainstream, we have ample opportunity to mess with people. . . . So far, we've done it in a classy way — we made music we like that's weird, but it also got picked up on the radio. . . . There are so many clichés we can fall into. An ultimate goal is not to become a douchebag."

—Andrew VanWyngarden of MGMT, *Spin*, November 2008

I WAS 22 YEARS OLD when I first learned the sting you feel when your self-image is altered in the blink of an eye. Pierre and I were standing unsteadily on the back bumper of a motor rickshaw as we tore down a dirt road in Bihar, and Pierre said what he did. My head did not feel like it was spinning, so much as reconfiguring itself from the inside out, at great speed and with considerable damage, as it must feel to undergo an Ovidian transformation.

A soldier finds out the war is over; a prisoner becomes a free man; a former president leaves office;

all three stare out a window and realize, with a growing sense of dread, that they are no longer equipped
for life back home. In my case, I learned that I come off
as a douchebag.

Multiple connotations clicked through my head:
a guy I knew in high school who nicknamed himself
"The Hammer" and got laid off from Bear Stearns; a
summer's breeze through feathered, shoulder-length
brown hair and the words "Sometimes I just don't
feel fresh, even *after* a shower"; Jägermeister; toothy
smiles; Jimmy Fallon. "Sort of a douchebag." "A *real*
douchebag." "That fucking *douche*bag."

Pierre and I were living with other students in
a monastery in northeast India. There were no tele-
visions or computers or even radios allowed in the
monastery so when we weren't writing by candlelight
about Pratītyasamutpāda or eating or meditating or
sleeping, we played chess, traded books, and talked.
A favorite topic of conversation was our impressions as we first appeared to one another in the
London airport. Where there was so much talk of
deconstructing identity and fostering an understanding
of no-self, and with a shaved head and more or less
identical clothes, it was easy to forget who you had
been back home. And yet it still wasn't altogether
comfortable for me that, upon first laying eyes on me
at Gatwick — me, in a button-down shirt and a hat
(non-Castro, non-trucker, non-porkpie), with short

hair and friendly Midwestern sensibilities — Pierre's brain had flashed:

DOUCHEBAG (VAR.: FRATTY DOUCHEBAG)

We all know where the epithet originates; it refers to a soiled object, a private shame. According to *The Oxford English Dictionary*, the term "douche bag" was first used to refer to something other than a female cleaning implement some time in the 1960s, when it was used to describe "an unattractive co-ed," or "by extension, any individual whom the speaker desires to deprecate." Other sources imply that the term originally indicated a woman of "loose moral repute." Where the term leaped across the gender gap from denigrating unattractive women to describing contemptible men remains unknown.

In the 1980s, the term seems to have been popular among young teens as a blanket insult — used for example to disparage a priggish teacher that one did not like — though it lacked any attached cultural codes. It is perhaps in a sense of '80s-inspired nostalgia that the term was resurrected in the early 2000s, along with various other appurtenances from that era.

Reviewing the earliest 21st-century literature on douchebags, the word in its early revival seems to describe a certain kind of male — juiced, gelled, bronzed, plucked, collar-popped — who is stereotypically thought to have originated in or near New Jersey, but who, sometime around 2002, suddenly begins popping up everywhere. As this type hardened into the New Guido, the word escaped and articulate definitions became more difficult. "You know one when you see one," ran the tagline of Obvious Douchebag, one of the many new douchebag-focused blogs on the internet. The expansion marked a turn in meaning, as well as the word's quick devaluation and fall. By 2008, a rash of hip publications were already declaring the word "dead," among them *Esquire*, *SF Weekly*, and Gawker.com (twice). Wrote one reader to the Gawker editors:

> [The word "douchebag" has] been completely played out. the number of times i hear it now applied to any circumstance other than what i believe to have been its true intention is getting annoying. furthermore, i feel the douche's [sic] themselves have co-opted the word and use it against hipsters and the like. people who aren't particularly witty, or even funny, began throwing around the word douche (in my opinion denigrating the original beauty of what it represented).

The expansion of meaning that this class of commenter seemed to be picking out for "douchebag" (now deprived of its "original beauty"!) was not the "Jersey Boy" at all, with his long history of derogatory names before douche: "townie," "tool," etc. Rather, to Gawker and to the likes of *SF Weekly*, the douchebag had represented the antipode to the hipster. And more than that. Like "douchebag," "hipster" was a name that no one could apply to oneself. But the opportunity to call someone *else* a "douchebag": that offered the would-be hipster a means of self-identification by a name one *could* say, looking outward. In the douchebag, the hipster had found its Other.

S INCE INDIA, I HAVE been called a douchebag no less than six times by hipsters. On one occasion I asked a 19 year-old RISD student if I was *acting* like a douchebag. No, you're nice enough, she said. But you're wearing a collared shirt, and loose jeans, and that's what douchebags wear. "I bet you even have abs," she said.

Like a hermit crab, the mainstream is in the process of sloughing off one aesthetic and adopting another. It picks up what the hipsters leave behind. I imagine it felt similar in the mid-1970s, when hippies' shaggy hair and mustaches became mainstream grooming, or in the mid-1990s when the sweatshop clothing market started manufacturing Seattle grunge flannel. The wheels are in motion again now: the Jonas Brothers are wearing keffiyehs.

More and more, young television characters resemble people I thought were hipsters six months ago — chronically undernourished, seasonally over-dressed — and writers have conspired to surround them with a dummy army of douchebags. The arch-douchebag is for me best typified by Andy Bernard (played by Ed Helms) from the NBC version of *The Office*. You can read him from his smirk — that unique mixture of unflinching entitlement, measured success, and undue self-worth. When he opens his mouth, his words only confirm what his posture tele-graphed. "I went to Cornell. Ever heard of it? Yeah, I graduated in four years . . ." But you might argue that the biggest douchebag is actually Michael, the tragic corporate clown who travels to New York to eat a slice of Sbarro pizza, or the bespectacled, cardigan-wearing Ryan, a burgeoning "hipster douchebag" — which is to say, yesteryear's hipster. Part of the show's genius is that each character represents a different facet of the hateful mainstream, which correlates to figures in our lives. Which you perceive as true douchebags, well, that depends on whom you identify yourself *against*.

The great majority of douchebag theory published on the internet is penned by professed fans of the word, those who apply it liberally and with a certain sense of vindictive glee. Occasionally the message reaches its intended prey. "So I started Googling myself, you know," said John Mayer, to a TMZ cameraman, "And I had to kinda put it all together at once to realize, at the end of it all, *I'm kind of a douchebag*."

He is, almost definitively. One month after staring into our cultural lens and conceding he was a douchebag, Mayer took to his blog to defend himself, not by denying the label, but by disassembling it. In his ham-fisted analysis, Mayer posits that the epithet is applied out of jealousy, or a sense that fame has been dealt to the undeserving. "Is being a douchebag actually all about having a bigger smile than someone else deems you deserve to in life?" he asks.

Such a question would earn Mayer the title all by itself. But one hears the plaintive cry beneath it. Above all else, the douchebag believes he seeks a kind of legibility, or in simpler terms, *normalcy*. Don't chicks dig smiles, guitars, and shiny fabrics? If you listen to his judgments of others, the douchebag reveals that, above all else, he strives not to be "weird"; in fact, not to be labeled at all. Who strives for something so mundane? In a culture where normalcy is as quicksilver and fleeting as ours, where trends seem to shift at an ever-increasing rate, and norms are demolished and reconstructed yearly — in a culture such as this, achieving a state of normalcy can be a kind of triumph.

The famous douchebag arrogance comes with the false assumption that normalcy has been achieved *and that it's a true triumph.* The douchebag who considers himself "relatively normal" thinks he is speaking from a centralized location, a place of authority. To the outside observer, however, he simply looks mediocre and smug.

And indeed, why should the douchebag be humble? He is at the center and apex of all things. The average American douchebag is a model citizen of our society: masculine, unaffected, well-rounded, concerned with his physical health, moral (but not puritanical or prude), virile without being sleazy, funny without being clever or snide; he is at all times a faithful consumer, an eager participant, and a contributor to society. He buys what the mainstream tells him to buy; he listens skeptically to the current hits and reverently to the hits of the past. In all respects he is the Hegelian synthesis of the '60s culture war: taking bong hits during timeouts in the Packers game, he keeps his eyes on a flashing advertisement for the Marines. If he is high (or poor) enough, who knows, he might just enlist. He is everything he has been taught to be; he does everything society asks of him. And for all of this effort, he assumes that he will be granted a slight, unspoken modicum of respect and admiration.

Yet this respect — respect predicated upon normalcy rather than uniqueness — is exactly what the hipster withholds. Only in this way can the hipster maintain his complacency, believing he deprives some douchebag of his. But when douchebags have discovered skinny jeans, as they surely will . . . with what will the hipster then cover his pale, skinny ass? Parachute pants?

YOU KNOW IT WHEN YOU SEE IT

WHAT IS THE "hipster feminine," and why are attempts to define it so unsatisfying? Reach for names, and you wind up with artists — claiming as icons of hipsterism those accomplished women of this and past generations who appeal to hipster taste: in painting, Elizabeth Peyton; on film, Chloe Sevigny; in music Karen O., Kathleen Hanna, and Kim Gordon, representing the '00s, '90s, and '80s, respectively. There's Deanna Templeton, Beth Ditto, Joanna Newsom, Björk; even crowd-pleasers Zooey Deschanel, Diablo Cody, and MIA. But you can't in earnest call these women hipsters, save in wanting to knock their particular achievements. Their honest roots lie elsewhere — so they don't quite fit the bill.

Almost by definition, real hipsters are *not* artists. They're curators and critics, re-mixers and designers, the copywriters and "prosumers" who trail in the artists' wake. At best, it seems, they're art students: aspiring cultural savants who collect the names and slogans of past avant-gardes to hoard or brandish conspicuously, like capital.

Or — in the case of many women — like *clothes*. It's telling that once adopted or sanctioned by hipster taste, those would-be exemplars of the hipster feminine are not praised for their art, but repurposed as style icons: Chloe Sevigny for Opening Ceremony, Chan Marshall (a.k.a. Cat Power) for Chanel. Karen O. of the Yeah Yeah Yeahs has contributed as much to culture with her haircut as her music — a hairdresser in Los Angeles once told me that "the Karen" was briefly a mid-aughts answer to "the Rachel" — and Enjoy-your-style.com now celebrates Kathleen Hanna of the riot grrrl band Bikini Kill for outfits that were "fun, even sexy" — words unlikely to please the composer of "Suck My Left One" and "Resist Psychic Death." Even Jenny Holzer has a line for Keds: a set of monochrome canvas high-tops that plead, in sans-serif all-caps emblazoned across the heels, "PROTECT ME FROM WHAT I WANT" — $75 from Bloomingdales.

It points to an unsatisfying partial-truth: that the female hipster's privileged knowledge is not subcultural, intellectual, or even pseudo-intellectual, but the familiar "female" knowledge of how to look. Knowing when side bangs have given way to short bangs or when lace-up dress shoes have usurped casual slip-ons doesn't work within a power structure to push against its walls. If anything, it fortifies that structure from the inside, providing it the braces and supports — exclusivity, envy, aspiration — that sustain the fashion industry.

If women disappeared in the conversation that sought to articulate male hipsters — the one that noticed men dressing differently, adopting funny style markers like tight pants and cardigans that signified a shift in identity — it's likely because the people having that conversation saw (and maybe see) no novelty in women dressing to fit a culture. The reduction of female artists to "it girls" only seemed to confirm the sense that clothing *was* women's true culture, their familiar domain. This line of thinking saw the phrase "hipster female" as a redundant banality, and the women who walked arm-in-arm with Williamsburg's hipster men merely variations on fashionable, non-hipster women. It assumed, in other words, that a "true" hipster female didn't exist: if hipsters were fashion victims, then all women were hipsters, and therefore none were.

This of course isn't true — we all know hipster women, and non-hipster women. For both sexes, hipsterism is mostly a play of surfaces, a game of outward signification (a hipster is someone who looks like a hipster; "I know it when I see it," as Justice Stewart said of obscene pictures); but whereas the hipster male could be pinned down by a set of simple cues, the hipster female receded into a network of complex signifiers — and so those of us looking for hipster women in sartorial details were looking in the wrong places. Ultimately, it seems to me that the physical appearance of the female hipster mattered less to her definition than the *presentation* of that appearance, and the media she chose for that self-presentation.

I'd argue that for the hipster female of 2004 onward — the one that emerged when I started paying attention — those media were party photography and self-photography, the two amateur forms most championed by the hipster. At the height of her fame, authenticity, desirability, specificity, inventiveness — her "roundness" as a character — the female hipster existed before the camera, photogenic and photographed; and so it was here, through the lens, that the hipster feminine came into definition. She may have remained a muse and a subject, flattened and available for exploitation. But if so, she was a muse for herself, and for other women.

TRACE THE ORIGINS of the hipster photographic aesthetic evinced by party- and self-photography, and all roads lead back to the Polaroid. In the work of the decade's most noted hipster photographers — Terry Richardson, Juergen Teller,

Dov Charney, the late Dash Snow — need it be said all men? — even those photographs shot on digital or traditional film clung to the Polaroid's visual vocabulary: over-exposed flash, a risqué amount of flesh, a thin palette of muted ambers and blues. For its characters the hipster aesthetic took pale, slender-thighed women with tousled hair and smoky eye makeup — models plucked from the Polaroid casting-call portrait — and prop men who, if dressed at all, dressed for the medium: athletic socks, white tees, tight-fitting pants, and mustaches, as if stepping into the Polaroid frame meant stepping into the styles of the '70s.

The Polaroid SX-70 was released in 1972, the only mass camera before the digital that could do what the new technology does: render photographs that were both instant and private. The years in which digital cameras were becoming cheaper, more accessible, and good enough to compete with film led up to the Polaroid Corporation's bankruptcy in 2001, and its ultimate discontinuation of instant film in 2008. There were plenty of new things you could do with the digital medium's differences (Photoshop distortion not the least of them), but for hipsters, tying the new, cheap, and soon-to-be ubiquitous medium to a rare and dying form was preferable. With its roots in basement porn, modeling headshots, and crime scene photography (Polaroid integral film required no additional processing; the image couldn't be tampered with or enhanced), the look of the older stock seemed to imbue all subjects with a sexy authenticity. It spoke to the hipster moods of irony and nostalgia, the hipster fetishes of obsolete media and tactile souvenirs. But best of all, it offered paradoxical claims to a lo-fi rawness and the possibility of self-construction — that ability to watch one's own image appear on film, and then adjust, and shoot again — for which digital media had whet the appetite. Even amateurs could stage "spontaneity" in two dimensions, looking as one had when passively, unfakeably "captured" by the camera.

And then there was Andy Warhol, that illegitimate father of hipsterdom. Warhol all but disappeared at parties "unless he was taking pictures with his Polaroid camera," as fellow photographer Burt Glinn recalled; and for all the talk today of his postmodernism, Warhol's photos and films were works of obsessive authenticity. Each Polaroid and screen test suggested the presence of a real person on the other side of the camera, alive at a unique moment and manifesting herself for a merely recording lens. Transvestites, starlets, addicts, socialites, hustlers — they turned gruesome rarity into glamour. *Life was like this*, Warhol's camera declared, and after him the Polaroid seemed inextricable from such claims. Riding on Warhol's legacy, Polaroid-wielding aesthetes of later decades sought similar intimacy and glamour in the New York club scene. And thus, in 2004, hipster party photography was born.

THAT YEAR, celebrity photographer Jeremy Kost found "inspiration in the eclectic and gritty characters of New York's famed underground East Village and Lower East Side," and began snapping real Polaroids of hipsters and the "fashion elite" to scan and display on his website, RoidRage.com (tagline: "Where Life Becomes Art"). Also in 2004, Mark Hunter, a Los Angeles-based party photographer known by his online handle "The Cobra Snake," started to capture a younger set of raucous, bicoastal hipsters for his own website, PolaroidScene.com. (Hunter later renamed the site "The Cobra Snake" after receiving several letters from Polaroid's legal department, which claimed his photos of wasted, underfed rich kids and tattooed scenesters were tarnishing the brand. "[They said] they would sue my ass if I didn't stop using the name," Hunter told an interviewer for the self-described taste-making site TheBrilliance.com. "The good thing is now I'm better off. People would always say, 'Hey, that's not a Polaroid camera.'")

Last, and perhaps most famous of the Polaroid-inspired hipster photo blogs, was LastNightsParty.com (also 2004), brainchild of the Canadian musician Merlin Bronques, who claimed in his artist bio, "Photography is more rock and roll than rock and roll is."

Bronques was infamous for donning a glossy wig and sunglasses at night (a Halloween costume-cum-Warhol homage, as Melena Ryzik noted in a 2005 *New York Times* article), and for coaxing salacious poses out of attractive, inebriated women at high-profile New York parties. Like Kost and Hunter, Bronques photographed celebrities, socialites, twentysomethings, and the new "gritty characters," self-conscious performers who populated the social demimonde — drag queens, porn stars, and burlesque performers.

Most of the events captured by all three photobloggers were corporate brand-sponsored after-parties held at major venues — a launch party for Sony PlayStation; another for the British clothing company Ben Sherman; another for Patrón tequila. But for Bronques and Hunter, occasional photos of a friend's birthday party or a day trip to a "hip" neighborhood offered more offbeat illustrations of how hipsters spent their time. The girls always looked good, if a little dead in the eyes. Not everyone was a famous person, but everybody looked like one.

While neither Bronques nor Hunter ever shot Polaroids (both used, and still use digital cameras), Last Night's Party and The Cobra Snake themselves retained something of the Polaroid's evidentiary power. As early as 2005 both sites were being cited as hipster notaries: grace these virtual pages and you were "officially" a hipster (went the logic), and upon that principle further claims of identification or disavowal could be built. Carles, the mystery blogger behind the pop-sociology website HipsterRunoff.com, once denied (and confirmed) a certain level of hipsterdom, stating: "I have only been on cobrasnake 2 times + last nights party 1 time." A little differently, the web-trawling bros who documented their study of "The Game" on the seduction forum RooshV.com settled a debate over whether "hipster chicks" were "hot" enough to warrant their use of mind-control techniques by agreeing to look at photos on Last Night's Party. (The verdict: hipster women could "be hot — really hot," but exacted hidden costs: "I don't feel like sitting around talking about The Arcade Fire and Andy Warhol all night.")

The seducers were right to point to these sites for their hipster definition, since from them emerged an image of the female hipster that was remarkably stable and distinct — varied as the women who embodied it doubtless were beyond the camera's field of view. The hipster female was thin, and often had bangs; she wore red lipstick and horn-rimmed glasses, leather jackets and second-hand dresses. But more consistent than her outfits were her poses: placed before the camera she stared right into it — either disaffected, or deer-in-headlights — or, tilting her chin down to one shoulder, mustered a thoughtful pout or puckered lip. Then sometimes she got up on a table, took off her pants, stuck out her tongue, or downed a 40 while collapsing into a crowd of revelers. Mostly, though, she just stared, unsmiling, looking seductive, or bored.

From these postures emerged intimations of a personality. Dozens upon dozens of party photos testified to the essential "chillness" of the hipster female — whether that meant "chill" with smoking American Spirits on a stoop with Vincent Gallo, or "chill" with taking off her shirt for strangers. (Toplessness remains a major trope on Last Night's Party, as essential, in a way, as it is to *Girls Gone Wild*.) Hipster women could also be, as one Gothamist blogger put it to Bronques in an interview, "hot/interesting" — but never hot/interesting at the expense of being chill. Mark Hunter once said his favorite girls were "girls who sit on the floor, who have a relaxed attitude about things," and that his favorite photographs were "pictures of skinny girls who sit on the floor." And so these were the photos his audience saw: pictures of hundreds of chill, skinny girls, sitting on the floor.

HUNTER'S IDEAL of hipster chillness was perhaps best embodied by Cory Kennedy, his one-time girlfriend, intern, and muse, who was perhaps the most iconic hipster female to be born of aughts-era party photography. Kennedy was Hunter's Edie Sedgwick, an effortlessly photogenic teenager whom he met, as he recounted in a *LA Times Magazine* feature, at a Blood Brothers concert at the El Ray when she was only 15. As he began to take her to parties and feature her in his photos, Kennedy became famous for being famous, especially among the computer-bound suburban girls who loved her simply for looking the way she did: pale and skinny with tangled brown hair, poky elbows, bruised knees, and waxy, hooded eyes. She wore tattered black tights and chunky jewelry up her arms, would sit down on any floor and do goofy, childish things, like play with her food or stick out her candy-stained tongue while those around her rubbed traces of coke from their nostrils and tried to look sexy. Whenever Hunter posted pictures of Kennedy on The Cobra Snake, web traffic spiked. Mostly, Hunter told the *LA Times'* Shawn Hubler, "from fashion community sites."

So Kennedy, too, became a style icon, not only in the US but also in places like Holland and Argentina. She inspired legions of young women around the world to try out their self-photography in her image, and they did — displaying their results on social profiles, LiveJournals, and personal blogs. On dating sites like Nerve.com and in eBay vintage "stores" — where entrepreneurial ladies modeled and sold the fashions proffered by hipster photo blogs with searchable titles like ***VINTAGE HIPSTER INDIE BOHO FLORAL-PRINT ROMPER CORY KENNEDY!!!*** — self-photography became a way to privately test out oneself-as-hipster, to hide under bangs and sit, in tattered tights, on the pavements of one's own neighborhood.

At the peak of Cory-mania in 2006 or 2007, self-photography was already a familiar cultural practice, as essential to the construction of an online persona as a list of one's favorite movies, books, or people. And so the hipster female's self-construction dovetailed with the existing habits of the mainstream, where people were already in the middle of figuring out how to package and present themselves for others. The internet, after all, was not for hipsters alone.

But if the female hipster of four or five years ago once set herself apart with self-portraits that subscribed to the hipster aesthetic — blinding flash, dead-on stare, off-kilter angle, or Cory Kennedy outfit — today she's among the majority. This past June, the *New York Times* ran an article in Fashion & Style offering tips for self-photography (now a more widespread phenomenon, argued writer David Colman, thanks to technology like the self-facing iPhone camera) with the assistance of DJ/hipster photographer Rachel Chandler. The accompanying slideshow of Chandler's self-portraits, entitled "This Years Model: Me," spells out the canon of hipster self-photography in terms so explicit it's jarring.

Captioning a white-bordered photo of herself reclining in Ray-Bans and a bikini beside an empty Polaroid cartridge, Chandler says: "If you are going to go to all the trouble of using a real Polaroid instead of mocking it up with Photoshop you should definitely put some proof in the picture." Beside her flash-lit glamour shot under some bougainvillea, in the next slide, the *Times* narrates: "Many people try to deal with a cheap flash by turning it down or off, but Ms. Chandler points out that turning it up is a good option. It blows out wrinkles and gives the photo a modern look, especially with a little over-the-top vamping."

I T WAS ONLY after Roid Rage, The Cobra Snake, Last Night's Party, and Cory Kennedy — and after the self-photography that aped hipster aesthetics and proliferated on social networking sites — that I began to see hipsters at my own high school, in Los Angeles. And only after them did I begin to see skinny jeans, horn-rimmed glasses, vintage dresses and beat-up flannel shirts displayed with unthinkable price tags, not in Jet Rag or Aardvarks or the other "vintage" haunts, but in the floodlit windows of Beverly Hills boutiques — far from the burgeoning hipster enclaves of Silverlake and Echo Park. It was as if the hipster feminine had finally been distilled and packaged by so many photographs, and logically ascended to high-end women's fashion — only to trickle down again, through Urban Outfitters, Forever 21, and Target.

The more time that passes, and the more photographs of hipsters that pop up on blogs like "Look

At This Fucking Hipster" and user-generated fashion websites like Lookbook.nu — where girls (and boys) model and photograph hip outfits for other users to "like" and rank — the more it seems that the hipster female born in 2004 was purely the invention of photography, filtering down to us who at the time were still 15. As is true of many fantasies involving women, photography was the only place where the hipster ideal of a child-bodied beauty having an outrageous good time, flitting pensively through industrial wastelands or "ironically" playing on a history of sexual subjugation by posing naked for a clothing company could actually exist.

Perhaps better this life, performed for the camera, than the one young women were actually living: clocking hours at some underwhelming marketing or retail job, skipping meals to afford (and fit into) overpriced vintage clothes, meeting guys in noise/indie/art-rock bands who turned out to be feckless losers. Maybe moving back in with one's parents, or — if one was lucky — making some art and getting some attention. Where Warhol's photographs laid claim to a certain reality, the hipster female's party- and self-photography professed a willful artifice. *Life isn't like this*, the photos seemed to say. *But can't a girl dream?* Of the party scene, Kennedy told the *LA Times*, "It came off more wild than it was."

EPITAPH FOR THE WHITE HIPSTER

A T THE START OF the great blackout of August 14, 2003, radio announcers on every battery-powered transistor in every knot of bystanders in New York City recalled with apprehension the looting that had appalled the nation during the blackout of 1977. Darkness was falling again upon the metropolis — now a post-Disney wonderland which had parlayed the white return and gentrification of the 1990s, plus the harsh policing of "Giuliani Time" and chief cop William Bratton, into a money boom that persisted, with falling crime rates and still-rising real estate valuations, even after the disaster of September 11, 2001. Had the stumbling-block arrived at last? Fourteen hours later, after the sun rose over intact shops, authorities were jubilant. The neighborhoods of Crown Heights and Bushwick, where the worst trouble transpired a quarter-century earlier, had stayed calm. No looting had occurred. Or almost no looting, certainly not enough to matter to anyone, not in Manhattan — really just one set of incidents that newspapers bothered to record, and *that* was just something that happened to some Lower East Side hipsters.

The chief venue was a store called Alife, pronounced "A-Life," as if bestowing a superior grade on your existence. It called itself a brand- and design-consultancy, but was known primarily as an unaffordable sneaker store, selling limited edition Nikes or customized Chuck Taylors, improbably expensive — up to $800, at the high end — amidst peculiar decor: trick bikes, motocross jackets, astroturf, graffiti paints. From the day it opened on Orchard Street, an anomaly on the block, it made me uncomfortable to see, in much the way that conservatives who speak of "white culture" make me uncomfortable. After successes, it added a hidden exclusive club, decorated like a Savile Row tailor's, to vend sneakers to patrons unintimidated by the absence of a phone number, a Tiffany's-style buzzer, a signless barred steel door, and "members only" stationary. Alife entered a neighborhood that was Puerto Rican, black, and Jewish, on the street traditionally known for bargain leather-goods and clothes — but from 1999 onward it became the western pillar of a swiftly-growing enclave of new people whom I never heard called anything other than "hipsters," carved out from Orchard via Rivington (where the sneaker "club" opened), east to Clinton, where a celebrated, unaffordable restaurant had opened (59 Clinton Fresh Food),* also serving wealthy patrons who arrived by cabs or town cars and looked bemused when they stepped onto the sidewalk.

A little before 11 pm on the first night of the 2003 blackout, thieves broke open a side trash-area door of the Alife club and a significant crowd began looting the stock. The owner arrived and hit shadowy people with a flashlight to disperse them; the mob struck back with 40 oz. bottles. This is, of course, a sneaker neighborhood. What Alife had pioneered was the up-pricing, super-branding, and remarketing of products more or less on sale right around the corner at the famous discount sneaker shops on Delancey, like Jimmy Jazz and Richie's, serving a mostly black and Latino clientele — but Alife addressed a non-local or tourist market, trading on the novelty of an impoverished location still within the confines of Manhattan. No trouble was recorded at Jimmy Jazz or Richie's; a brick was thrown through the window of the Delancey Foot Locker, and another Foot

---

* Wylie Dufresne, not yet a Food Network celebrity, apparently opened his restaurant here because he had grown up in the neighborhood — a not infrequent reason for the first "pioneers" to merchandise an area to which rich people didn't previously travel.

Locker was burglarized in Brooklyn. At rich white people's sneaker destinations throughout the hipster archipelago in the Lower East Side, however — Alife's imitators: Nort on Eldridge, Classickicks on Elizabeth across the northern border at Houston, even one shop called Prohibit, as far west as the part of Little Italy rich brokers had recently renamed "Nolita" — attacks, attempts, and thefts were reported, the only notable crimes of the period of darkness.

MY SENSE AT THE time was that the neighborhood had taken a kind of revenge, pathetic as it was — and all the more shameful, since two of the broken bottles at Alife led to stitches. It was the only revenge, however, or gesture of rejection, I ever knew the neighborhood to take. And how much rejection can there really be, in trying to grab by force the unattainable goods on the other side of glittering windows?

My vantage was unusual, biased in two different directions but well-suited to amateur sociology. My father's family had been living in apartments near Willett Street, on the east side of the neighborhood, continuously since the turn of the century. My grandmother and father had been spinning stories of those streets for me since I was a kid — overwriting the visible neighborhood, a mix of tenements, workers co-ops, and public housing, with specifics of what had been there formerly. So I was attached to the patterns of settlement. Through the period of the changes taking place on the opposite side of Delancey from my grandmother's apartment, I visited a few times a year for stays occasionally as long as a month. I gawked in the box of streets that made the epicenter for the new culture, bounded by Houston to the North, Delancey (later Grand, after the expansion) on the South, Clinton to the East, and Orchard (later Allen) to the West. I went there first at an age when I still desperately cared what "the young people" were up to — and nearly all the people I saw were then older than me. I read hipster catalogs and fliers, visited their stores, chatted, and took notes.*

A word on the "old neighborhood" bias: when I was a child visiting in the '70s and '80s, I got used to those streets as my grandmother and father experienced them, because of the way "the street" experienced us — as poor Jews, basically Orthodox, among poor Puerto Ricans and poor blacks. It was a flatter

---

* Though I've tried out rival definitions for "hipster" elsewhere, this article uses the term without qualification, to build up the word's meaning in historical context. Even where this usage seems different from the reader's own, it may, in the end, become compatible.

The question remains of how the name arose. I'm certain I knew to call the new migrants "hipsters" from the first time I explained to my family the changes happening north of Delancey in the late 1990s, and before hearing anyone else use the word. If true, this means it was possible to read the term off of hipsters' appearance and behavior. "Hipster" referred, in part, to an air of knowing about exclusive things before anyone else — that they acted, as people said then (and

distribution, where my family was taken for granted and was embedded. It excited me unduly, and at the same time I found it relaxing, a relief, to escape where I actually came from — I know such emotions are suspect. My father, who had classed our family up by going to college and moving to white-collar jobs, saw me as naïve to like rudeness, dirt, and especially public housing, which since 1965 had been an affront to the family not only for the racial and religious confrontations it brought but because it leveled the tenement in which my grandfather was born.

To enter the hipsterized area to the north in 1999 was to be treated again as what I was in the Boston suburbs where I actually came from, namely, an entitled white person among entitled whites. Our class likes to call itself middle-class, as everybody in America does — but as I kept arguing to my no-longer-working-class father, we were *rich* just to live in Newton. The income distribution nationwide at that time

---

do still), "hipper than thou." But I think it also must mean that circa 1999 their look was still continuous with the short-lived neo-Beat or '50s-nostalgic hip moment (with goatees, soul patches, fedoras, and *Swingers*-style duds) that the *Baffler* relentlessly documented and attacked as a marketing ploy through the 1990s. You can find the record of it in their anthology *Commodify Your Dissent* (1997). To summarize the derivation: I think the very earliest new hipsters may have looked enough like the old hipsters of dim mid-century memory to call up the name, reinforced by complaints about hip snobbery that were ubiquitous during the decade (cf. the August 8, 1994 *Time* cover).

showed a median family income of about $50,000 (it has stayed at that level, too, in the decade 1999–2009). On the Lower East Side, it was $28,000, with about 30% of families below the poverty line. The hipster whites were like me. It takes a very strong-minded person not to enjoy the restoration of privilege, and I happily went to Rivington Street to read in a new cafe, where, it should also be said, everybody was noticeably better looking than in Boston. At the same time, it would have taken a blind person not to see, as the bars and boutiques proliferated, and friends I knew from college told me they were coming to rent in the neighborhood, that the non-chain stores my grandmother had always depended on (Ratner's the kosher dairy restaurant, Friedman's where she bought clothes) continued to disappear, vanishing along with the Puerto Rican *cocina frita* stop on the corner of Clinton and the other stores affordable to my grandmother's Orthodox Jewish neighbors or the residents of the low-income Samuel Gompers Houses facing her building.

I'd never been so close to a neighborhood "in transition." But I also hadn't seen a transition quite like this. I knew bohemia. It was very clear to me that the hipster neighborhood was not a bohemian neighborhood; it wasn't artists. Artists were occasionally there — drinking coffee — but they were unusually thin on the ground. Instead of doing art, people everywhere were "doing" products. They displayed overpriced guitars, overpriced painted-upon sneakers, lots of overpriced foods, and a huge quantity of overpriced clothes. These products were often displayed amidst the decor and signifiers of art galleries or designer's hidden ateliers, but artistic *production* and artists' folkways were gone. I kept walking into stores that I thought were thrift shops or Goodwill, which turned out to be curated or repurposed stores for vintage clothes priced higher than the brand new dress shirts I got twice a year at Filene's. Priced high enough, in fact, that it suggested I was in the presence of a much higher social class than mine, which was surprising because people lacked other clear markers of wealth. (Later I understood that the class that kept up appearances at street level might be funded by credit card debt and living paycheck-to-paycheck.)

Another crucial thing: hipster youth also wasn't punk, crunchy, DIY, rockabilly, ska, mod, or hardcore, which meant it wasn't in line with youth subculture as I knew it everywhere else. If the twin strands of US youth oppositional subculture run through punk and DIY on one side, and an environmental, anti-authoritarian tradition of stoners and jam bands and dreadlocks and vegans and, basically, hippies on the other side, and both these lines have cross-pollinated endlessly — all of it was missing. Then there were the offenses against taste that those other subcultures would never have undertaken, which made me *wish* somebody would put a rock through these windows. Traditionally the Jewish streets in the neighborhood had sold discount garments, hosiery, haberdashery, wholesale cloth, trimmings. Hipster boutiques liked to keep the old, now ironic signage with Jewish names — as hipster restaurants kept signage from replaced Puerto Rican and Dominican restaurants in Spanish. I found this obscurely enraging, like setting up a lemonade stand on someone's grave. Worse, hipsters developed a trend of not putting names on their restaurants or bars at all, giving everything an exclusive and unwelcoming aspect; as if an average passerby was not invited to come in and have a beer.

This subculture was pro-consumer, pro-consumption, amoral, pro-lifestyle. It credentialed itself as resistant because its pleasures were supposedly violent and transgressive (I knew this from *Vice* magazine, a free fashion-boutique publication) and also what was then foolishly called "politically incorrect," such that the hipster's primary means of self-authentication were white hetero masculinity, gross high school pranks, and, primarily, pornography. What pretentious erotica had been to '60s liberals, pretentious porn was to '00s hipsters. Oh, and tattoos! Everybody claimed to have a background in punk/skateboarding/graffiti to justify why they were now in retail sportswear and marketing. Drugs were authenticating, too, but drugs of course are the one thing that almost every American youth subculture loves, from hipsters to hippies to jocks, not excluding gamers and wenches at the Renaissance Fair. The big publication of the early hipster moment was called *Vice* precisely because that was the hipster shtick, to lump consumer and Gothic into the same category of transgression: We will show you how to buy pleasures which some liberal prude of our fantasies considers immoral; thus our publication will be a chance for naughty boys to have their own *Redbook* and look at one another in fashion spreads. Its most famous department was a Dos and Don'ts. If the hipster then spent $1000 on clothes, or a painted skateboard, or Johnny Walker Blue Label — it seemed like rebellion.

Friends told me to visit Williamsburg, Brooklyn, which was the true center of hipster development at that time, and maybe more bohemian-friendly. I made two treks there on foot across the Williamsburg Bridge around 1999–2000, passing through the not-yet-changed southlands to reach Bedford Avenue. I found Bedford incredibly unnerving, a zombie-village of people like me, more conspicuous where the buildings are so much smaller and sparser than in Manhattan. It was as if the hipsters had taken over Gopher Prairie.

ABOVE ALL, THE THING I chafed at, mentally, was that the hipsters manifested in these neighborhoods not like a subculture, but like an *ethnicity*. It's hard to explain. Their structure of behavior, what one can only call their "clannishness," plus the Lower East Side's hands-off treatment of the new hipsters — as individual blocks and then whole streets "turned" — seemed like consequences of new ethnic arrival. The hipsters' secrecy contributed, too. If they didn't label their stores in Yiddish or Spanish, they telegraphed their distinction by a kind of rich-people's invisible ink. Hipsters had no obvious exchange with the groups around them, entirely unlike the way artists I had seen elsewhere liked to join into neighborhoods of racial others — whether to integrate or "slum," exploit or make nice. I learned to give directions in a new way to people near my grandmother's house, looking for Chinatown: "First you go through the Puerto Rican part, then the hipster part, then the Jewish part, and *then* it's Chinatown."

The markers of hipster ethnicity were straightforward. They were coded "suburban white." In those key early years, the hipster aesthetic drew from 1970s suburbia (the decade, importantly, that had turned its back on both the city and the counterculture '60s, as well as the decade in which these hipsters had been kids) and 1970s amateur porn (the secret rebellion supposedly going on underneath the suburbs). Bars

dug up white Americana, as at the pioneering Welcome to the Johnsons (1999) on Rivington Street — its
conceit was that you were drinking in a family's 1970s
middle-American living room. "Trucker hats," the
gimme caps distributed as freebies at auto shows
and worn throughout the country, occasionally worn
through the punk years as signs of downward-mobil-
ity or just the towns bands came from, were newly
discovered for fashion. (One landed on Paris Hilton's
head.) Belt-buckles got Southern and big. "Wifebeaters" — the same athletic tank top undershirts worn by
Puerto Ricans and Dominicans on nearby streets, but
not with that name — became chic. The open secret
of the equally famous "ironic" T-shirts, printed with
mottos from community pig roasts, church softball
leagues, and Midwestern car dealerships, was that
these shirts often came from people's own childhood
bureaus, especially among the middle-class young
people who had moved to New York from Tennessee,
Colorado, or Wisconsin (by way of college) to tend bar
on the Lower East Side while trying out art or work.
The rich were buying these shirts for $30 down the
street, and you already had them in your closet for
free. Thus middle-class whites helped to re-import
a white "opposite" culture to city living, "ironically,"
with an equivocal meaning. As did the Fruit of the
Loom undershirts when they represented a fantasy
about one's own tough white-ethnic grandfather, in

the suburbs after white flight, his simulated pissed-off ethos now brought back to the city.

What did this early hipster aesthetic mean? I was stunned when I read the conclusions drawn by John Leland in his massive history, *Hip*, in 2004. "[T]here's a broader, more interesting context for the emergence of Caucasian kitsch," he wrote (broader, that is, than continuity with the long history of '40s and '50s hipsters) because, Leland explained, it came along with "the most diverse, multicultural, middle-class, and ethnic-marketed generation in American history," when "one in five Americans is now either an immigrant or has a foreign-born parent":

> In this spirit, the trucker hat and other post-hip accessories play with the meaning of whiteness in a multicultural world. They make white visible. Without the black/white dichotomy to anchor it, and without numerical dominance to give it weight, whiteness is up for grabs. Especially in cities that are now 'majority-minority,' or less than half non-Hispanic white, whiteness is no longer the baseline, something taken for granted; it's something to be explored, turned sideways, debated for its currency. . . . Caucasian kitsch—which includes redneck rock, wife-beater tank tops, homey Little League t-shirts, corn dogs, drag racing, demolition derby and *Vice* magazine—packages whiteness as a fashion commodity that can be

donned or doffed according to one's dating needs. Post-hip treats whiteness the way fashion and entertainment have historically treated blackness. It swaths white identity not in race pride but in quotation marks. Whiteness doesn't define you, you define it—and you don't have to be white to wear it.

This feels to me like America as known to someone who doesn't leave the house. "[Y]ou don't have to be white to wear it?" That was true, but just about everyone I ever saw wearing these accessories on the Lower East Side was Caucasian, with the exception of a few Asian hipsters. Many of the latter, however, were actually from Asia. They were the ultra-rich young of Japan and Korea buying hipster brands. The few African-Americans I saw outfitted in Caucasian kitsch were mostly either celebrities on TV or models in clothing catalogs.

THE DEMOGRAPHIC SHIFT that concerns me more was the return of rich whites to big cities in the '90s and '00s and, with it, the suburbanization of poverty. When you think of the post-World War II decades, you think of suburbanization, "urban renewal," and "white flight," and its consequent defunding of the inner city. A common explanation for the looting and violence in 1977 in New York, indeed, is the fact that in 1975 the city had nearly gone bankrupt and economic opportunity and social services had been stretched too thin in the neighborhoods that rioted. The reverse phenomenon in our own times — after decades in which upward mobility for the middle classes, including the black and minority middle classes, had looked like it meant heading out to the suburbs — is that capital flowed back into the center, especially the finance capital of neoliberal upward redistribution and the 1990s and 2000s Wall Street bubbles. Little people were pushed outward to suburban housing, then hit particularly by the collapse of the real-estate-lending bubble that had generated the huge finance profits (with no penalty for the financiers; the US government bailed them out). The somewhat astonishing fact, for those who've watched the "rebirth" of the cities or their representations on TV, is that US poverty has been *rising* since 2000, according to US government statistics. The total number of the impoverished in suburbs now surpasses the numbers in the cities those suburbs serve, as well as housing the majority of the nation's poor overall.*

Especially in global cities (New York, Paris, Mumbai, London, Beijing), districts which previously

---

* This development was widely reported in 2010, but the turning point seems actually to have occurred slightly earlier in the decade. See Elizabeth Kneebone and Emily Garr, *The Suburbanization of Poverty: Trends in Metropolitan America, 2000 to 2008* (Washington, DC: Brookings Institute, 2010).

had historically not ever been of interest to the rich — because on the periphery of the city center (Lower East Side), or on the leading edges of the boroughs or commuting districts (Williamsburg, Dumbo), where these places were needed to house waves of servants, workers, clerks, small tradespeople, and immigrants — came into focus as sites for capital, valued as new leisure, entertainment, and to a lesser extent residential zones for the rich (wherever "luxury condos" could be installed and small dwellings broken into much larger spaces). Industrial and proletarian architectural detail, not accidentally, came to seem superbly charming, with the collusion of intellectuals sympathetic to and nostalgic for a working class. Whenever the richest didn't displace the poorer classes personally, too, they pushed what the sociologist Jean-Pierre Garnier terms the "inferior fringes of the intellectual petite bourgeoisie" out to poor neighborhoods — publicists and media hacks, teachers and professors, social workers, writers, all overeducated and with a psychic investment in hipness to compensate for their inferior real capital. This middling class of the educated classes accomplished the displacement of the working classes whose tenement façades they could lovingly restore.

The uncanny thing about the early-period white hipsters is that symbolically, in their clothes, styles, and music and attitudes, they seemed to announce that whiteness was flowing back in. Unconsciously, they *wore* what they were in structural terms — because for reasons mysterious to the participants, those things suddenly seemed cool. And by taking up the markers or feeling of a white ethnicity, they made it feel natural to engage in a subcultural separation, or de-integration, rather than bohemian integration, as they colonized neighborhoods that were, in one way or another, really ethnic — even when the people they put pressure on, as in the northern reaches of Williamsburg, were Polish.

I N AN EARLIER contribution, I mentioned what I think is the best anatomization of post-World War II hipsters, a 1948 article about black hipsters by Anatole Broyard.* The article is occasionally cited by historians but not widely enough known. Broyard saw hipster style, consciousness, and even snobbery, as the creation of a fictitious, independent base of power to rival white domination. The black hipster made pretense of a special superior truth that no one else could equal even had he possessed the same facts or abstract knowledge —an *a priori* knowledge comparable to the positive knowledge that whites held. You can see how this whole mood could attach itself to be-bop in the '40s, which was a true art and skill that was too fast,

---

* See "Positions," in this volume.

too complex, and too subcultural for whites yet to steal (as whites had taken over "hot" jazz and then big band and swing, while originators of those musical forms couldn't even perform as equals in many Jim Crow-era venues). Even the black hipster's now-forgotten early style cues seemed to evince a power to drag white knowledge into blackness, to see the white world, as it were, darkly. Recounted Broyard: "[The hipster] affected a white streak, made with powder, in his hair. This was the outer sign of a significant, prophetic mutation. And he always wore dark glasses, because normal light offended his eyes." Yet Broyard, a high-cultural re-appropriator or demander of white knowledge, on the model of Ralph Ellison, despaired of the power of style cues alone. If outsiders couldn't understand the black hipster, Broyard saw clearly enough, they would just move in to entrap and exhibit him: "He was bought and placed in the zoo," Broyard declared flatly. The only solution was true Promethean theft, stealing back the culture from whites that, in fact, African-Americans had helped create.

Of course, by 1957 Norman Mailer could publish his embarrassing declaration in "The White Negro" of the white hipster freeing himself from white squareness by Negro sexiness, spontaneity, naturalness, etc. Enough has been written about that odd essay not to expend more words on it here. What I've never seen noted anywhere is the extended letter to the

editor that ran in *Partisan Review*, protesting Broyard's article from the point of view of a white hipster,
three months after the article appeared *in 1948*. This
letter-writer claims that Broyard is a joykill to be so
serious and over-intellectual about a phenomenon
that's basically for kicks, and is already a hipster scene
for *whites*, who come to the jazz clubs and join in the
knowing fun. This is true co-optation: to make every
development "white" from the first, and to insist that
everything is style and style is meaningless. "You find
many hip studs, a great many Jewish boys again," he
says. "The white streak [in African-American hair] is a
purely theatrical gesture and is matched up by the blue
side-hair of various blond hipsters."*

Whenever a phenomenon like the hipster is read
for meaning, someone will deny it that meaning — the
white letter-writer to *Partisan Review*, and some hostile readers, I imagine, of this essay. Those who do
are often the ones who have an *investment* in these
actions not meaning anything — because evacuation
of meaning allows one to pursue the course without
scrutiny or self-reflection. If I read in too much significance to the white hipster moment of trucker hats,
Pabst Blue Ribbon, and belt buckles, I do expect objections of this kind — that it's a question of over-reading,

---

* I've wondered if it could be a joke, connected to the odd signature,
"Miles Templar." But it would have to a very, very sarcastic and unusual
joke on the white hipsters, not hinted at by other extra-textual cues.

not documentation. That's why it seems worth raising again the tasteless but factual issue of the connection between elements at the core of the 1999–2003 hipster moment and right-wing attitudes.

It was the *New York Times* that finally reported in 2003 the persistent connection of *Vice* magazine, and particularly its most voluble editor, Gavin McInnes, to unlikeable attitudes about race. The magazine had always made hostile jokes and used epithets about feminists and gays. Vanessa Grigoriadas for the *Times* dug into the reality of the attitudes, and concluded that they were real. She quoted McInnes: "I love being white and I think it's something to be very proud of. . . . I don't want our culture diluted. We need to close the borders now and let everyone assimilate to a Western, white, English-speaking way of life."

Grigoriadas then pointed out to readers an essay McInnes had published earlier that year in Pat Buchanan's *American Conservative* on how *Vice* was helping to confirm young people in the turn away from '60s liberal follies. Was this a prank? But it followed an even odder article *Vice* had published on their own ethos, which they called "The New Conservatives," combining it with a fashion spread no different from any other in the magazine. Whatever was true of *Vice*'s attitudes, you can feel their essential confusion and error in an interview from the previous year's *New York Press* with two of *Vice*'s three editors,

McInnes and Suroosh Alvi, that seems more or less sincere:

> [Interviewer:] *Vice*'s approach to homosexuality and race isn't traditionally punk rock.
>
> GM: The punk rock-ness of that is just plain honesty. We seem really racist and homophobic because we hang around with fags and niggers so much. It just becomes part of our vernacular.
>
> SA: Also, in '94, when these magazines were coming out, the political correctness in North America was overwhelming. Especially in the academic settings we'd just come out of. So we were reacting against that.
>
> GM: I think we got pissed off only after we wrote what came naturally to us and it offended people. We were determined to leave it in. It was just the way we talked. It's surprising how brainwashed by hippies most of our generation is. Pro-love, pro-diversity, pro-tolerance— that's the hippies' bag. You want to hear people talk about niggers, try hanging around with black people. They are harsh. You want to hear anti-Semitism, go hang around with some Jews. You should hear Suroosh talk about fucking Pakis. It's ear-burning. I'd argue that racists like the KKK don't really have anything to say about niggers and fags because they don't know any. They don't go, "I am so sick of fucking drag queens. They are so self-indulgent. Fashion this, fashion that. Can't you talk about politics for one second, you fuck-

ing transsexual?" They don't know. We're in the thick of it.

You see the mistake: being "in the thick of" industries tolerant of gays and Jews doesn't justify you thinking of them as fags and greedy Jew bastards. Only later in the interview does the line appear for which McInnes was ultimately criticized — when asked how *Vice* could bear keeping their offices in Williamsburg where there were so many post-collegiate wannabes, he replied: "Well, at least they're not fucking niggers or Puerto Ricans. At least they're white." I find it vaguely plausible, as McInnes protested to the gossip website Gawker.com, that aspects of each of these episodes were jokes and publicity stunts, and particularly that he wanted to scandalize the *New York Times*, which he counted on Gawker to hate along with him.

The thing about jokes, though, is that they do let you see where people's minds characteristically go, what it is they play with, when they reach the borders of social familiarity. For Norman Mailer, a self-proclaimed sexual ideologue and a leftist of varying types (sometimes a radical, sometimes a "left conservative" opposed to over-hygienic technocracy, but a man always alive to democracy of an essentially sensual, corporeal, Whitmanian kind), any effort at scandal took his mind toward miscegenation. He wanted, at least, to exalt something other than himself, combine, and disaffiliate from the whiteness he was bored by.* If Mailer was foolish when he wrote "The White Negro" — and he implied a decade later in *The Armies of the Night* that his black friends had told him, after the essay, that he was a fool — at least he was a fool who clumsily championed the violation of racial and class boundaries. In contrast, something in the "white hipster" imagination moved inexorably toward justifying rich whites in not having to be anything but white. Hipsters rationalized white colonization and separation by unconsciously forming an ethnicity for themselves (not connected, either, to the national-linguistic European ethnicities that lie behind Swedish Day or St. Patrick's Day or the Feast of San Gennaro). Hipsters worked this magic to keep themselves from feeling compromised, where compromise would have meant being obligated or connected to anyone among whom they might settle, Puerto Ricans or blacks or Jews or Poles or just people without money.

---

* Mailer was also Jewish, at a time when being Jewish did not make one fully white, and yet he had experienced a class rise, from ghetto Brooklyn to Harvard to old-boy literary life, which was unusual and just newly becoming available to Jews. In his mature career, he went out of his way to embrace the obscene and the "vital." Mailer thus offers an interesting test case for the contradictory class and racial positions available from mid-century to the present, and he, too, happens to have been viewing much of it from the (then predominantly Jewish) Lower East Side — he lived on Pitt Street in 1952.

I KNOW THAT THIS EARLY hipster culture, in its aspect of an aggressive fetishization of whiteness, ceased to exist. You could feel it coming to an end in 2003 — the sneaker-shop looting is a convenient symbol, but it really felt more like a loss of creative energy on the Lower East Side than a reaction from neighbors, like a tire draining of air. Hipsters clearly persisted and regrouped, though, with different markers and habits, in similar neighborhoods, and then in wider circles mediated by television and the internet.

The trouble is, I personally don't really know what hipsters 2004–2009 were like. The reason for my ignorance is aging. I mean: I got old. I turned 30, which seems as good a marker as any for a kind of electrified fence, running through the life-course, which can keep you out of subculture. Thirty is the age above which the '60s suggested nobody should be trusted. I did keep walking the same streets of the Lower East Side, and I could identify hipsters. I just couldn't see them with the same level of detail, nor did I understand the new fashions.

The reason isn't hard to guess, though it's not flattering for me. It must have been that I, like other people my age, was losing the compensatory benefits that an investment in hipsterism confers. If I didn't gain from knowing the codes, it's natural I would cease to see them or invest in understanding them.

Think about the ages at which subculture begins and ends for people. The essence of subculture is distinction. It can give a positive profile to unavoidable experiences of difference; you may join subculture when you are philosophically or ideologically out of step with the mainstream, or in some way handicapped in the dominant mainstream social competition. One easily understands why such forms of distinction take hold in high school, from ages fourteen to eighteen, and are valuable there. Your deficit becomes advantageous, if for nothing else than as a grounds for group solidarity. The loser who failed to make the football team becomes a skater; the nerd becomes a gamer; the leftist becomes a punk. In all sorts of frightening total institutions ruled by arbitrary authority, inmates will form groups for mutual defense and esteem, and then engage in inter-group rivalry and hierarchy. They persist to a greater or lesser extent in college depending on the specific structures of each institution.*

At age 22, however, when ambitious post-collegians travel to central metropolises, subculture can

---

* Students at smaller institutions of higher education are more likely to reflect, already, a single coherent class stratum (in background or aspiration) attached to a high social status with shared goals, and thus to experience slighter differentiation by subcultures. Larger institutions with wider class spread will encourage more persistent subcultures, except where the task of sub-grouping is taken up by an organized mainstream structure like the Greek system.

take on a new role. Many experience a sudden *declassing* in cities relative to college and even high school. The young graduate comes from a high status position but is suddenly without income and has no place in a city indifferent to college hierarchies. He or she still possesses enormous reserves of what Pierre Bourdieu termed *cultural capital*, waiting to be activated — a degree, the training of the university for learning tiny distinctions and histories, for the discovery and navigation of cultural codes — but he or she has temporarily lost the *real* capital and background dominance belonging to his class. Certain kinds of subculture allow cultural capital to be re-mobilized among peers and then within the fabric of the "poorer" city, to gain distinction and resist declassing.

Hence the meaning of the (not literally true) assumption that "all hipsters are rich": the truth it speaks to is the knowledge that, income-poor though they may be temporarily, young people who choose and can afford to pursue this form of status competition often have, at the least, been recipients of significant educational investment (leading to the college degree) and are likely to have possessed some safety from their previous, parental class status (a reliably middle-class backstop). Soon enough they are likely to ascend out of the poorer, low-rent neighborhoods in which they temporarily live. As for those ambitious people who move to the city from lower-middle-class backgrounds, the hipster mode equally provides worthwhile distinction in a cultural effort at classing up; you blend in and gain a new taste of future superiority. Superiority over other classes than your peers, too: you may be tending bar, but if you are tending bar in hip clothes and you're in a band at night, you'll always possess higher status in *culture* (if not in income) than the bond-trader losers ordering vodka tonics in button-downs.

The significance of age 30? A large percentage of those urban post-collegians, interning at some non-profit at 22 or 23 (or still planning to produce art or literature), by their experience of loss of status learn the superior economic rationality of trying to recover their earlier class positions by reentering conventional white collar work. Thus every micro-generation will be surprised by the number of its members who have been secretly preparing law-school applications while making fun of rich people who wear suits. Once these peers have a law degree and enter a firm — or, say, more generally, once many postgraduates have risen a bit, over five or eight years, within other chosen professions with middle- or upper-class remuneration (maybe they worked at these jobs all along, but dressed modishly) — they will have gained the means to compete and exploit the benefits of the metropolis on traditional grounds of income and class dominance. They take up more expensive and higher-class mainstream cultural distinctions (European-made cars, four-star restaurants, home mortgages). They fall out of subculture and fall upward into the mainstream.

When I look, in my blind way, at the hipsters of 2004–2009, a few things do stand out. The return of music — and a particular pattern of significance in the hipster music — crops up. I've said that early "white hipsters" were painfully unmusical, but the bands they did create pastiched previous white rock. This included bands like the White Stripes and The Strokes.* The music that hipsters listen to post–2004 seems to have a different mood, and here are the names of some significant bands: Grizzly Bear, Panda Bear, Deerhunter, Fleet Foxes, Department of Eagles, Wolf Parade, Band of Horses, and, behind and above them, Animal Collective. I watch their videos and enjoy a

---

* One is tempted to say: The *White* Stripes! Jack "*White!*" This aesthetic of Classic Rock-friendly blues was being produced in indie circles at the same time by a band calling itself The Black Keys, and both were pleasing in the way good cross-racial pastiche is agreeable when the original will never return again (cf. Winehouse, Amy). The moralistic question, as always, is whether the outcome of that racial crossover is cooperation or annexation. I prefer the former. (Thus I feel better about Amy Winehouse and her mostly black American or black English collaborators than about Jack White.) Also, imitating the "difference principle" in John Rawls's theory of distributive justice, we might ask whether the crossover pastiche benefits black musicians and music *first*, by producing renewed access to the culture of the dominant, before it benefits additional white pasticheurs. But such questions are notoriously difficult to judge and many find them offensive.

certain atmosphere of pleasant orgy, with traces of psychadelia; hear animal sounds, and lovely Beach Boys harmonies; see unlocalizable rural redoubts, on wild beaches and in forests, in a loving, spacious, and manageable nature. And so many of the bands seem to dress up in masks or plush animal suits.

This would have been just a blip of pop culture — but then, in dress, post–2004, one saw flannel return, both for men and women; women took up cowboy boots, then dark-green rubber Wellingtons, like country squiresses off to visit the stables and the gamekeeper. Scarves proliferated unnecessarily, somehow conjuring a cold woodland night (if wool) or a desert encampment (the keffiyeh). Then scarves were worn as bandanas, as when Mary-Kate Olsen sported one, like a cannibal Pocahontas, starved enough to eat your arm. Hunting jackets in red-and-black check came back briefly.

It thus looks from the outside, both in music and in style, as if the post–2004 hipster turn has included an embrace of animal primitivism. Maybe also, in other clues, a kind of technological reduction. The youngest subcultures seem to know that the internet is convenient and also that the internet is a nuisance. In defiance of those graduates of the earlier hipster generation who, aging, retooled themselves as messianic internet-fetishistic prophets and publicists ("it'll change everything!"), children born as the '80s advanced seem to have seen their birthright in perspective. The ability to take the internet for granted, with its now complete penetration of life, led to compensatory reductions elsewhere. The most advanced hipster youth suddenly even deprived their bikes of *gears*. As CDs declined, LP records gained sales for the first time in two decades — seemingly purchased by the same kids who had 3,000 downloaded songs on their hard drives. The fixed-gear bike now ranks as the most visible urban marker of hip besides the skinny jean, and not the least of its satisfactions is its simple mechanism, and repairing it.

We'll have to wait and see whether the animals and fixies represent the spirit of a way out of a world of endless consumption and waste, resource depletion, environmental disaster, and the idiocy of internet messianism. Those we disparage as hipsters may represent just the least conscious, most consumerist tip of subcultures that may have richer philosophies and folkways — I hope so. I wish I knew the history of how Williamsburg after 2004, which felt like it had degenerated into a land of yuppie ex-hipsters having babies, got re-peopled with new 23- and 24-year-old bike-fixing hipsters who, to their credit, partly exiled the mombots and old, tattooed dads to the quieter precincts of Brooklyn Heights, Clinton Hill, or Park Slope.

What happened to the Lower East Side, meanwhile, I can attest: bigger capital moved in. The core hipster area very quickly entered capitalism's replica phase, in the pattern of postmodern development whereby originals are destroyed or priced out of an area beloved for its authenticity, so that mainstream pastiches can be installed with wider appeal, higher prices, and greater profitability. Thus, once kosher Ratner's closed in 2002 after nearly a century in business, the restaurant producer Keith McNally installed Schiller's (2003) one block north, replicating the look of an imaginary antique establishment from the neighborhood, but serving nachos. Coinciding with this was the arrival of high-rises and luxury residences: the out-of-place Blue building (2006), then the gigantic and numbing Hotel on Rivington (2005; beds for $820 per night) and Ludlow luxury apartment complex (2008). This was the phase of classic destructive gentrification, coming after hipster colonization. The hipster-coded kids I talk to now in cafes on the Lower East Side inform me they commute in from Bushwick or Bed-Stuy, to visit or jerk coffee in "their favorite place" that still reminds them of what they thought New York was going to be like when they arrived.

My hope is that amidst whatever sources of energy outside him- or herself the hipster no doubt continues to draw upon and advance, the self-satisfaction with whiteness, at least, will have somehow diminished — even if the Other whose blood hipsters suck isn't a trucker, but an imagined wild animal or an off-the-grid monkeywrenching hermit. If this consumerist culture of the hipster does survive and change, in the hopeful age of Obama, then even if it's still buying something, maybe it will buy something better.

SOUTH SIDE STORY
Hasidim vs. Hipsters

"The figure of the woman assumes its most seductive aspect as a cyclist. . . . In the clothing of cyclists the sporting expression still wrestles with the inherited pattern of elegance, and the fruit of this struggle is the grim sadistic touch which made this ideal image of elegance so incomparably provocative to the male world."

— Walter Benjamin, *The Arcades Project*

"This is our shtetl, and our walls must go high."

—Grand Rebbe Zalmen Teitelbaum, Satmar Hasidic leader

NEAR THE END of *Who Framed Roger Rabbit*, after Roger, Jessica, and Eddie are captured by weasels and delivered to the Acme factory, Judge Doom, the film's malefactor, reveals his plan to exterminate the inhabitants of Toontown. His objective, expressed in contemporary terms, is nation-building. And his means of ethnic cleansing? "Several months ago," Doom declares, "I had the good providence to stumble upon this plan of the City Council's. A construction plan of epic proportions! They're calling it a *freeway*." In 1988, when the film came out, public works had lost their power to awe, but Doom, speaking in a fictionalized 1947, was right to get caught up in reverie. Toontown would be rubble, its infrastructure swapped for "eight lanes of shimmering cement running from here to Pasadena."

The Bloomberg administration's 2008 commitment to build a 14-mile *greenway* connecting Bay Ridge and Greenpoint in Brooklyn — roughly the distance between Pasadena and West Hollywood — differed from Judge Doom's plan in some particulars. Instead of the gas stations, motels, fast-food hubs, and "wonderful, wonderful billboards!" that Doom giddily anticipates, the Mayor's cycling agenda envisaged an urban arcadia punctuated by sleek commutes, elfin waistlines, and extravagant landscaping. Just as in Paris, where a fashion-forward bike-lending program enlivened the presidential prospects of the sprightly Bertrand Delanoë, so, in New York, would the dwarfish Michael Bloomberg ride the two-wheeled wonder to the summits of environmental stardom.

By the summer of 2009, Bloomberg's transport chief, Janette Sadik-Khan, was already crowing, somewhat implausibly, that New York City had become "the bicycling capital of the United States." If the administration's ecotopian hard-liners got their way, the city would soon boast a cycling culture to rival even the extremist enclaves of northern Europe — Amsterdam, Berlin, Copenhagen — where cowed locals live in terror of importuning bike bells, the streets hostage to biker autocracy.

But first Bloomberg had to win reelection. In the months before the vote, Chinatown residents started complaining about a bike lane installed on Grand Street, asserting that speeding bicyclists posed a danger to ambulating oldsters. Truckers in Staten Island responded even more furiously, clinging to their vanishing parking spaces and chasing down any bikers who got in their way. The most intractable objections came from South Williamsburg, where the Satmars, a sect of Hasidic Jews, complained that a freshly consecrated bike lane on Bedford Avenue drew in a bad element: irresponsibles who flouted traffic laws and imperiled the neighborhood's many schoolchildren, who had to ford a river of cyclists when descending from the district's Hebrew-lettered school buses. The Yiddish-speaking Satmars referred to these unruly passers-through as *"Artisten."* The rest of the city called them hipsters.

HIPSTERS HAD THEIR OWN ideas about what was rankling the Satmars. As early as 2003, Williamsburg's Hasidic population had protested against a wave of so-called "yuppies," Manhattan transplants who brought high rents and loose morals. At a community board meeting, Hasidic participants denounced an expensive development on Broadway, in the shadow of the Williamsburg Bridge, as "an extension of the East Village," and a 21-year-old Hasidic attendee warned of "a very liberal lifestyle." "We have Jewish housing, synagogues, a Jewish medical center," he pointed out. The newcomers favored "bars and swimming pools. We don't like these things." A rabbi cast doubt on the new residents' "morality," deeming them "dangerous to our children."

Four years later, as land prices crept upward amid upper-middle-class youth migration, bike lanes came to South Williamsburg. At another board meeting on September 8, 2008, Hasids called on the city to remove new bike lanes on Wythe and Bedford Avenues and to postpone construction on a planned lane for Kent Avenue. Although the Hasid opposition presented several rationales for opposing the lanes, including, once again, the safety of children exiting school buses and the loss of parking spaces, the most explosive motive was articulated by board member Simon Weisser, who told the *New York Post* that he was perturbed by clothing. "I have to admit, it's a major issue, women passing through here in that dress code," he said. "It bothers me, and it bothers a lot of people." To hipsters, this showed the Satmars' true colors — they were oppressors! That very summer, the Satmars had complained about a billboard visible from the Brooklyn-Queens Expressway featuring the swim-suited cast of *90210*. Earlier in the decade, the community had been similarly aggrieved by a billboard for *Sex and the City*. The Satmars weren't worried about safety, they were worried about erotic danger. And if the Satmars wanted to make this about sex, then sex was what they'd get!

The city's Department of Transportation, observing events from its headquarters on Worth Street in lower Manhattan, suddenly found itself cast in the role of a colonial viceroy forced to adjudicate between warring indigenous tribes. Of course, neither of the Williamsburg disputants could be classed "indigenous" in any rigorous sense — the Satmars began to arrive in the late 1940s, the hipsters in the late 1990s; and, really, tribes at least usually share some common history, some deeper connection to a region. Maybe the hipsters and the Hasids started to seem more like cartoons.

A FRIEND OF MINE, raised in a Reform Jewish household, likes to joke that the most transgressive thing she could do would not be to marry another woman, or get addicted to heroin, but to become a

Hasid. Satmars don't proselytize, but Lubavitchers famously do, and one of the reasons America's Hasidic population has grown so dramatically in recent decades is that they've found converts among once-secular Jewish youth.

There's a logic to this. At their most extreme, hipsters and Hasids present rival heresies, dueling rejections of bourgeois modernity. That each group selected Williamsburg as the terrain for carving out a secessionist utopia can only be blamed on the cunning of history, plus the L train.

The symmetry is powerful, if accidental. Both factions are marked by recognizable hairstyles and unusual modes of dress. Where the hipster wardrobe is ever-changing — one day it's trucker hats, overalls, and chin straps, the next it's fedoras, onesies, and bangs — the Satmar uniform has proven stable over 70 years: white shirts, pants, three-piece suits, shtreimel fur hats, and *payes* side braids for the men; shin-length dresses and sumptuous wigs for the women. Both groups are resented by their near relations (ordinary bourgeois youth, mainstream Jews) for their economic dependence on others — hipsters on their parents and/or arts and non-profit funding, and Hasidim on charity: despite pockets of wealth, one third of Hasidic families in Williamsburg receive some form of public assistance.

Both groups live in configurations unusual for the advanced capitalist west. Hipsters often live with multiple roommates, encouraging a wide variety of romantic, or worryingly platonic, entanglements. Hasids live in enormous families. The *average* size of a Satmar family is nine people. It would not be unusual to enter either a hipster or a Satmar apartment and see a cot in the kitchen.

For all its medieval costuming, Satmar Hasidism is a relatively recent phenomenon. The various Hasidic splinter groups — Lubavitcher, Satmar, Belz — trace their roots to the mid-18th century, when the mystic rabbi Israel Ba'al Shem Tov gained a following for his anti-scholastic, kabbalistic revision of Orthodox Judaism. The Satmars, a large and particularly con-scientious division of Hasidim, were founded only in the 20th century, by Grand Rebbe Joel Teitelbaum, who would have been murdered by the Nazis had his freedom not been purchased from Adolf Eichmann by the Zionist Rudolph Kastner. Nevertheless, Teitel-baum hated the Zionists, even blaming them for the Holocaust.

Teitelbaum arrived in New York with a small retinue on Rosh Hashanah in 1946 (5707, on the Jew-ish calendar), where he founded a synagogue and set for himself the task of recreating the cloistered world of Satu Mare, the Hungarian shtetl whence the Sat-mars sprang. Fur hats, Talmud study, and procreation were the order of the day. From an original colony with a reputed population of only ten after World War II, the Satmar population in Brooklyn, bolstered by immigration, grew by 2006 to more than 35,000. Although parts of the community are plagued by poverty, the Williamsburg Satmars are better off than the co-religionists in the upstate refuge of Kiryas Joel, which is often called the poorest place in the United States. The downstarters got into Brooklyn real estate before several rounds of booms, and they also entered the traditional diamond business.

The Satmars speak Yiddish to each other. Their major paper, *Der Yid*, has a circulation of 50,000, roughly on par with the *London Review of Books* (about half as many as *Vice Deutschland*). Hipsters, too, have long evinced an affection for Yiddish, especially when combined with accordions, as in Klezmer music. Franz Kafka, a significant hipster if not the original one, had a weakness for Yiddish theater.

Like other schismatic spin-offs, Satmars and hipsters have struggled to maintain unity in the face of generational succession. As Michael Powell reported for *New York*, the death of charismatic founder Rebbe Joel in 1981 left the Satmars looking to his nephew, Moses Teitelbaum, to take the top spot. Although Moses never matched Joel's appeal, the community continued to grow and prosper. Moses' eldest son, Aaron Teitelbaum, seemed the heir apparent, but in his last months of life Moses decided to annoint his third son instead, Zalmen. Aaron cried foul, triggering repeated convocations of the Beis Din, the Satmar religious court. In 2006, the New York State Court of Appeals refused to help resolve the matter, calling the internal religious dispute "non-justiceable." Though less litigious, hipsters in Williamsburg have also been riven by inter-cohort tensions, as the aging early pioneers have added baby boutiques to Bedford Avenue, attracting the derision of younger migrants.

A MID THESE FEARS of community dissolution, rumors of bike lane confrontation began to swirl on both sides. Hipsters, for their part, started to resent the increasingly bellicose tone of epithets hurled at them on Bedford Avenue by angry, black-hatted pedestrians. Although the insults were delivered in Yiddish — Yiddish commanding much hipster enthusiasm but little comprehension — the cyclists got the drift. One familiar tale repeated in online cycling forums warned of a club-wielding bus driver who would chase and threaten to maim any hipster who complained about his parking job. Was the neighborhood lurching toward an anti-hipster pogrom?

One particularly terrifying legend featured a character referred to as the Ginger Hasid rapist. This tale, a bizarre hipster refraction of the Hasids' anxiety about over-sexed "artists," turned predator into prey.

In the story, a fresh-faced hipster ganymede returns to his rented room late at night and finds an obese, red-haired Orthodox visitor hiding in the closet. On discovery, the Hasid rapist attempts to kiss the boy, running away at the first show of resistance. That this shadowy figure was essentially non-violent, boy-friendly, and not actually a rapist at all, did nothing to reduce his fascination.

L AST NOVEMBER, BLOOMBERG squeaked into a third term with just over fifty percent of the vote. Four weeks later, the city announced its decision to remove fourteen blocks of bike lane from Bedford Avenue between Flushing and Division. Seth Solomonow, a spokesman for the Department of Transportation, described the move as "part of ongoing bike network adjustments in the area." Others described it as a quid-pro-quo, the fruit of a deal struck with Satmar leaders on the eve of the election. Solomonow encouraged bikers to use a new two-way lane on Kent Avenue and a barrier-protected connector lane on Williamsburg Street. A spokesman from the Mayor's office called the replacement route "the Cadillac of bike paths."

Initial hipster reaction was angry but peaceful. A group dressed as clowns led a funeral procession along Bedford to protest the decision, but failed to capture the public imagination since they lacked any vernacular of protest other than the language of a grant application. "Enforced, protected bike lanes save cyclist lives, improve the landscape and make better use of public space for most of the community," said the clowns.

Others tried action: they would repaint the bike path. The first repainting attempt took place in two sessions, one on Friday, November 27th — the Sabbath — and the second on Sunday, November 29th. The painters posted a video on YouTube documenting their rolling, spraying, and stenciling exploits. The video mimics the DIY-charm of *Trading Spaces.* Its hipster protagonists look handy and youthful. The sequence ends with a service announcement printed in four installments in stark white letters. "We are New York City bicyclists, and our message is clear: Don't take away our bike lanes./ We use this stretch of Bedford Avenue because it is a direct route to the Williamsburg Bridge./ We will continue to use it whether or not there is a bike lane there, but not having one puts us at greater risk from cars./ That's why bike lanes exist — for safety. Do not try to remove them, or we will put them back for our own safety."

Here the hipsters employed the unmistakable register of a teenager trying to "use reason" with adults. The strategy is to appeal first to safety concerns, then to the inevitability of transgression in the event of a ruling against the child.

Repainting was nearly complete when the hipsters met the Satmars' neighborhood vigilante unit, the Shomrim, who "bear-hugged" the vandals until the NYPD arrived. Although the police made no arrests that night, after the video posting and Satmar complaints, repainters Quinn Hechtropf and Katherine Piccoci were eventually arrested for "criminal mischief' and "defacing the street." Hechtropf, defiant in defeat, proclaimed himself a "self-hating Jewish hipster."

Escalating the conflict after the apprehension of Hechtropf and Piccoci, hipsters planned a naked bike ride along the old funeral route. Calling themselves "freedom riders," a group organized by Heather Loop, a 27-year-old bike messenger, arranged to meet at the Wreck Room, a Flushing avenue hipster redoubt, and ride together to the Williamsburg Bridge in underwear, breasts exposed. "If you can't handle scantily clad women," Loop told reporters, you should "live in a place where you can have your own sanctuary, like upstate." But Loop had the misfortune of selecting one of the coldest days of the winter. Attendance was low, and no one rode naked, though some riders pinned fake rubber breasts over their wool coats.

Hipsters then invited the Hasidic community to engage in a public debate. On January 25th, 2010, an open discussion was held at Pete's Candy Store on Lorimer St. — hardly neutral territory, which may have accounted for the fact that only three Satmars showed up, the activist Isaac Abraham and two adjuncts. As Michael Idov reported in an article for *New York*, Abraham held his own in an overwhelmingly biker-friendly crowd, speaking with conviction against disrespectful speed-demons (he revealed in the course of the evening that his wife had been the victim of a biker hit-and-run). The hipsters parried with their own horror stories, including the one about a bus driver with a club. At one point, an exasperated Abraham asked, "So in other words, what you're saying is I should go back to the community and say that I just got a message, it's their way or the highway?" To which the officially impartial moderator responded, "Their way IS the highway!"

After the event, a blogger on FreeWilliamsburg.com conceded that Abraham had seemed genuinely concerned about the safety of pedestrians, paving the way for a return to hipster placidity. During the debate Caroline Samponaro, an activist with Transportation Alternatives, had pointed out that bikers and pedestrians were *both* "awesome," and "should be working together, not against each other." Her solution, or her attempt at one, was to call for the establishment of "Waving Wednesdays," during which she would ride with a group of hipsters at rush hour through the zone of contention and wave at Hasidic pedestrians to "improve safety and morale" and foster a "positive, communal atmosphere."

THE DOÑA MARINA figure in this drama, who spoke not only to the demands of hipster and Hasid, but also, and most emphatically, to the demands of the press, is Baruch Herzfeld, a 38-year-old lapsed Satmar who runs a used bike shop called Traif Bike Gesheft — "the unkosher bike shop." Herzfed moderated the Pete's Candy Store debate, a position won on the strength of his reputation as a go-between. His Gesheft offered bikes to Satmar patrons at reduced prices. But Herzfeld sided with the hipsters during the bike lane controversy. He has been referred to as the "unofficial spokesman" of the repainters, although the extent of his involvement is unclear.

A couple blocks from Herzfeld's "Gesheft" is a pork-anchored restaurant also called "Traif" that caters to both hipsters and to Hasids on the down low. Predictably, real hipsters prefer Gottlieb's, the kosher Hasidic deli around the corner. In a *Wall Street Journal* article examining hipster/Hasid commercial exchange, a 25-year-old motorcycle-racing trust funder explained that Gottlieb's has "everything — good food, good prices, irony."

Up and down Lee Avenue, the Satmar SoHo, men charge along in pairs and children scurry, stopping occasionally to tug at their beleaguered mothers. Scattered through the neighborhood are well-trafficked playgrounds. There, little Satmars, boys and girls, run, play, scream and *ride* — wheeling around with impunity on a wide range of scooters, wagons, bikes, and tricycles: the mayor's cavalry-in-training.

Evidence of a thaw mounted throughout the spring. In May, the Sundance hit *Holy Rollers* premiered in New York, starring a side-curled Jesse Eisenberg as a young Hasid from Williamsburg who winds up working as an ecstasy mule in the transatlantic drug trade. Hipsters noted that Eisenberg's role was difficult to distinguish from the Jewish adolescent he played in Noah Baumbach's *Squid and the Whale*.

On June 27, 2010, the MTA enacted a package of alterations to New York subway routes with uncertain implications for the neighborhood depicted in Eisenberg's Hasid debut. The once-sleepy M train, which had been widely rumored to be slated for elimination, instead emerged a winner, annexing the V line and with it a direct route from South Williamsburg through SoHo, the West Village, and Midtown. The now-vanished Bedford bike lane had been used by hundreds of people every day. The M train is used by a hundred thousand.

Historically, a certain caliber of hipster always preferred South Williamsburg to its modish northern cousin, anyway — much as a certain caliber of Manhattanite has only ever been to South Williamsburg to dine at Peter Luger, the century-old steak house. Now Williamsburg's South-siders — hipster purists and Satmar worshippers accustomed to seclusion — will find themselves in one of the newly most convenient and underpriced neighborhoods in the one of the biggest and most covetous cities in the world. They should enjoy it while it lasts.

CONTRIBUTORS

JENNIFER BAUMGARDNER is a critic and co-author (with Amy Richards) of *Manifesta: Young Women, Feminism, and the Future*. Her most recent book is *Abortion & Life*.

JACE CLAYTON, better known as DJ /rupture, has written for *n+1*, *Fader*, and elsewhere. His most recent album is *Solar Life Raft*.

PATRICE EVANS blogs as The Assimilated Negro. His first book will be published by Crown/Three Rivers later this year.

CHRISTOPHER GLAZEK is a fact checker at the *New Yorker*.

MARK GREIF is co-editor of *n+1*.

ROB HORNING writes the "Marginal Utility" blog for popmatters.com and is an editor of The New Inquiry.

MARGO JEFFERSON is a winner of the Pulitzer Prize for criticism and most recently the author of *On Michael Jackson*.

CHRISTIAN LORENTZEN is the former film critic for *n+1* and currently a senior editor at the *New York Observer*.

ROBERT MOOR is a writer living in New York. A version of his essay "On Douchebags" originally appeared in issue 1 of Wag's Revue.

REID PILLIFANT is a staff writer for the *New York Observer*.

DAYNA TORTORICI is a writer living in Providence.

Special thanks to: Eugene Lang College, The New School, and Dean Neil Gordon; Carla Blumenkranz, Willa Cmiel, Kiera Feldman, Anna Feuer, Ashton Goggans, Ali Heifetz, Larry Jackson, Casey Blue James, Jennifer Riegle, Elizabeth Stark, and the editorial board of n+1.

BIBLIOGRAPHY

Baldwin, James. "The Black Boy Looks at the White Boy." *Esquire*, May 1961. Reprinted in *Nobody Knows My Name: More Notes of a Native Son.* New York: Dial, 1961.

Bourdieu, Pierre. *Distinction: A Social Critique of the Judgment of Taste.* Translated by Richard Nice. Cambridge: Harvard University Press, 1984.

Broyard, Anatole. "A Portrait of the Hipster." *Partisan Review*, June 1948.

"Correspondence." *Partisan Review*, September 1948.

Dewan, Shaila K. "With Lights Out, Looters Set Sights on Sneaker Shops." *New York Times*, August 18, 2003.

Ellison, Ralph. *Invisible Man.* New York: Random House, 1952.

Frank, Thomas and Matt Weiland, eds. *Commodify Your Dissent.* New York: Norton, 1997.

Garnier, Jean-Pierre. *Une violence éminemment contemporaine: Essais sur la ville, la petite bourgeoisie intellectuelle et l'effacement des classes populaires.* Marseille: Agone, 2010.

Grigoriadis, Vanessa. "The Edge of Hip: Vice, the Brand." *New York Times*, September 28, 2003.

Idov, Michael. "Clash of the Bearded Ones." *New York*, April 11, 2010.

Jameson, Frederic. *Postmodernism, or, The Cultural Logic of Late Capitalism.* Durham: Duke University Press, 1991.

Kneebone, Elizabeth, and Emily Garr. *The Suburbanization of Poverty: Trends in Metropolitan America, 2000 to 2008.* Washington, DC: Brookings Institute, 2010.

Lacayo, Richard. "If Everyone is Hip . . . Is Anyone Hip?" *Time*, August 8, 1994.

Lanham, Robert. *The Hipster Handbook.* New York: Anchor Books, 2003.

Leland, John. *Hip: The History.* New York: Ecco, 2004.

Lloyd, Richard. *Neo-Bohemia: Art and Commerce in the Postindustrial City.* New York: Routledge, 2006.

Mailer, Norman. *The Armies of the Night: History as a Novel, the Novel as History.* New York: New American Library, 1968.

Mailer, Norman. "The White Negro: Superficial Reflections on the Hipster." *Dissent,* Summer 1957. Reprinted in *Advertisements for Myself.* New York: Putnam, 1959.

McInnes, Gavin. "It's Hip to be Square." *The American Conservative,* August 11, 2003.

Perry, Charles. *The Haight-Ashbury: A History.* New York: Random House, 1984.

Powell, Michael. "Hats On, Gloves Off." *New York,* May 1, 2006.

Smith, Greg B. "Owners of Looted Store to Sue City." *New York Daily News,* August 19, 2003.

"The New Conservatives." *Vice,* August 2002.

"Vice Rising: Corporate Media Woos Magazine World's Punks." *NY Press,* October 8, 2002.

Weiss, Bari. "Hasids vs. Hipsters: A Williamsburg Story." *Wall Street Journal,* April 17, 2010.

XXL Staff. "Hipster Boogie." *XXL,* June 2008.

INDEX